Anonymus

Meditations for the young

Anonymus

Meditations for the young

ISBN/EAN: 9783741178597

Manufactured in Europe, USA, Canada, Australia, Japa

Cover: Foto ©ninafisch / pixelio.de

Manufactured and distributed by brebook publishing software (www.brebook.com)

Anonymus

Meditations for the young

MEDITATIONS FOR THE YOUNG.

REVISED BY A JESUIT FATHER.

January.

LONDON: BURNS AND OATES.
DUBLIN: M. H. GILL AND SON, SACKVILLE STREET.
Price Fourpence; or Three Shillings per Dozen.

Nihil obstat.

A. DIGNAM, S.J.

Imprimatur.

HENRICUS EDUARDUS,
Card. Archiep. Westmonast.

Die 30 Nov. 1870.

CONTENTS.

JAN.   **PAGE**

1. CIRCUMCISION OF OUR LORD . . . 5
2. THE VIRTUES THAT OUR LORD PRACTISED IN HIS CIRCUMCISION . . . 8
3. THE SAME (CONTINUED) 9
4. JESUS IS OUR SAVIOUR 11
5. LIFE OF JESUS AND MARY AT BETHLEHEM 13
6. THE EPIPHANY OF OUR LORD . . . 15
7. THE WISE MEN AT JERUSALEM . . 17
8. THE BIRTHPLACE OF CHRIST . . . 19
9. THE THREE KINGS AT BETHLEHEM . . 21
10. THE ADORATION OF THE MAGI . . . 23
11. THE THREE GIFTS 26
12. THE RETURN OF THE THREE KINGS . . 28
13. HOW WE SHOULD IMITATE THE WISE MEN 30
14. OUR LORD'S FIRST VISIT TO JERUSALEM . 33
15. FEAST OF ST. PAUL, THE FIRST HERMIT . 35
16. JESUS IS PRESENTED IN THE TEMPLE . 37

CONTENTS.

JAN.   PAGE

17. JESUS IS REDEEMED ACCORDING TO THE LAW 40
18. ST. PETER'S CHAIR AT ROME . . . 42
19. HOLY SIMEON 45
20. SS. FABIAN AND SEBASTIAN . . . 47
21. ST. AGNES, VIRGIN AND MARTYR . . 50
22. THE PROPHECY OF SIMEON . . . 52
23. THE ESPOUSALS OF OUR LADY . . . 55
24. THE PROPHETESS ANNA 58
25. CONVERSION OF ST. PAUL THE APOSTLE . 61
26. THE RETURN TO NAZARETH . . . 64
27. CHILDHOOD OF ST. JOHN THE BAPTIST . 67
28. OCTAVE OF ST. AGNES 70
29. ST. FRANCIS OF SALES 73
30. ST. MARTINA, VIRGIN AND MARTYR . 75
31. FEAST OF THE HOLY NAME OF JESUS° . 78

   * This feast being a movable one, we have thought it best to place the meditation for it at the end.

MEDITATIONS FOR THE YOUNG.

January.

JANUARY 1.

FEAST OF THE CIRCUMCISION.

Preparatory Prayer.

First Prelude.—Imagine you see the stable, now made somewhat less wretched.

Second Prelude.—Teach me, dear Lord Jesus, to bear pain patiently.

First Point.

Circumcision means cutting the flesh.

None of us can bear to see a little baby suffer pain, but our dear Lord suffered for love of us when He was eight days old. Instead of painful circumcision He gave us

Holy Baptism; and the drops of water fall softly on the babies' faces, for they are the figures of His Precious Blood.

Second Point.

Our dear Lady knelt by and saw the Blood flow. What terrible pain this was for her! Yet she did not grudge to us, her children, the Blood of her beloved Child. She offered up that first bloodshedding for our salvation.

How we ought to love our Lady, and how we ought to learn to love God's holy will! When we see those we love suffer, let us not complain, but adore God's holy, just, and divine will.

Third Point.

This is the first day of the year. Jesus gives to each of us a New Year's gift—His Blood, His Heart, His Tears, His Mother's tears.

Do you give Him in return your heart, your will, your love?

Here should follow a *Colloquy;* that is, you should try to speak to God in prayer, and you should make a resolution and offer it to Him; and if you pray to our Lady or the Saints or Angels, you should do the same. Here is an example of what is meant; but these colloquies, or conversations with God, must come from our own hearts in meditation, as they are different from the prayers we say out of a book.

Example.

Dear Lord, Thou didst suffer so much for me: give me courage to suffer a little for Thee. I am such a coward, so afraid of pain: help me, my Jesus. I want to begin this year well—to learn to love Thee more, to serve Thee better. I can do nothing without Thy help and grace. Help me, dear Lord, to overcome that fault . . . . . . which is so hard for me. By Thy grace I resolve this day to be patient with . . . . . ; or to obey that order to do . . . . . . which

I so much dislike. I will try and recall this thought during the day—the First Tears of Jesus.

January 2.

THE VIRTUES THAT OUR LORD PRACTISED IN HIS CIRCUMCISION.

First Prelude, as before.

Second Prelude.—Lord Jesus, give me grace to imitate Thee.

First Point.

In His circumcision our Lord practised obedience. He submitted to the law of the Jewish Church. Then how obedient ought not you to be to your parents, your teachers, your confessor—to all who have authority over you!

Second Point.

He practised humility because circumcision was the punishment of sin. He, the Sinless, the Divine, made Himself appear like a sinner; and you, who really are sinful, do you not often try to hide your faults, to excuse and disguise them? And are you not often vexed and angry when they are pointed out?

Third Point.

He practised mortification; He suffered pain for our sakes. So we, after His example, should be willing to deny ourselves, to give up a pleasure if it leads us to sin or imperfection. Every day each one should 'take up his cross'—that is, suffer something, deny himself or herself something, for the love of our Lord.

Colloquy.—Resolution.

JANUARY 3.

THE VIRTUES THAT OUR LORD PRACTISED IN THE CIRCUMCISION (CONTINUED).

First Prelude, as before.

JANUARY THIRD.

Second Prelude.—Teach me, dear Lord, to imitate Thee.

First Point.

Our Lord practised patience. He bore this sharp pain without complaint. It was a strange welcome from His people, and it was a foreshadowing of what was to come. All His wounds and sufferings were laid on Him by His people. And every fault of ours, even a little one, had its share in giving Him pain and causing His Blood to flow. Shall I go on committing them?

Second Point.

Our Lord practised love of retirement, love of the hidden life. He was circumcised like other children. He did not make Himself remarkable by claiming an exemption. All through His life our Lord hid Himself as much as He could. And do not we love to show ourselves off, to attract notice? Do we not sometimes do things that are really wrong from no other motive?

JANUARY FOURTH.

Third Point.

Our Lord practised self-sacrifice. He did this for the sake of others; He loved us better than Himself. How stands our love for others? Even for those we profess to love are we ready to make sacrifices? or does our love consist in sweet words and caresses, and nothing more? And do we try to conquer any feeling of natural dislike to others, remembering that our dear Lord loves all His creatures, and for all shed His Blood?

Do not begin the year with any grudge or feeling of dislike to another in your heart.

Colloquy.—Resolution.

JANUARY 4.

JESUS IS OUR SAVIOUR.

First Prelude.—Imagine you see our Lord in His Mother's arms.

Second Prelude.—Jesus, my Jesus, be to me a Jesus.

First Point.

God is with us; earth as well as heaven possesses His presence. He came from love, in love, to show His love. His little arms are open to receive us, to pardon us, to help us. O, then, let us trust in the Lord our God with great confidence.

Second Point.

How cold He was in the crib! Try to warm Him with your love. If you are humble and obedient and gentle, He will come to you, and you can hold Him in your arms. He 'giveth grace to the humble' (St. James iv.). 'He will teach the meek His ways' (Ps. xxiv.). To the haughty and disobedient He will not come near.

Third Point.

Our Lord wishes to bury all our sins in the depth of His mercy. He wants us not to be afraid of Him, but to come to Him to tell Him our faults, our fears, our troubles. What would you have done if you had really gone into the stable, and Mary had put her Baby into your arms? Do now, say now, what you would then have said and done.

Colloquy.—Resolution.

January 5.

LIFE OF JESUS AND MARY AT BETHLEHEM.

First Prelude.—Imagine you see the stable and the crib.

Second Prelude.—Jesus, Mary, and Joseph, I give you my heart and my soul.

First Point.

This poor stable is the house of God. Enter in, however, without fear. Listen to the sighs that issue from the Heart of the Infant Jesus. He does not mind His own sufferings. He sorrows to see the sins of men.

Let us try to comfort Him by doing all we can to please Him.

Second Point.

Our dear Lady saw her well-beloved Child suffering cold and privation, and was resigned. How fondly she tried to warm Him in her bosom! How she kissed and caressed Him, and pressed His Sacred Heart against her own! How close was the union between Jesus and Mary!

Let me try to unite myself to them, to bring my poor feeble heart and lay it at their feet.

Third Point.

Let us think how best we can imitate Jesus and Mary. We must be faithful in our prayers and spiritual duties, and we must be diligent in our daily tasks and occupations.

Jesus is no longer in the stable, but He is ever on the altar.

Colloquy.—Resolution.

January 6.

FEAST OF THE EPIPHANY.

First Prelude.—Imagine you see the star in the heavens.

Second Prelude.—'Show me the way that leadeth unto Thee.'

First Point.

'We have seen His star' (St. Matt. ii.).

A miraculous star had appeared in the East to announce the birth of Jesus Christ. Many saw it, but *three* only resolved to follow it and find the new-born King.

If our minds are filled with useless thoughts, if we will follow only our own way, we do not see the light God would give us, and thus we miss His grace.

Second Point.

'We have seen His star.'

How great was the mercy and love of God in calling these Wise Men, who were Gentiles, to behold the Messias! Gentiles were all those races and peoples on the earth who were not Jews; for the Jews were God's chosen people, and until the birth of our Lord the Jewish Church was the one true religion.

Reflect on God's goodness to you, who are in the bosom of the Catholic Church, the one true faith.

Third Point.

'We have seen His star.'

The Wise Men, having seen the star, rose up and followed it, leaving all things they cared for behind them.

Are you willing to make sacrifices for God? In the first ages of the Church even children laid down their lives for the faith; and in all ages, as in our own, even children are often called on to 'confess Christ before men.'

How often are Catholic children sneered at or laughed at by Protestant companions!

Then it is they must be brave, remembering that to them has been revealed the star of faith.

Colloquy.—Resolution.

January 7.
THE WISE MEN AT JERUSALEM.

First Prelude.—Imagine you see the crowded streets of Jerusalem.

Second Prelude.—' Show me the way that leadeth unto Thee.'

First Point.

'Behold there came Wise Men from the East to Jerusalem, saying, Where is He that is born King of the Jews ?' (St. Matt. ii.)

The journey of the Wise Men is a type of our journey to our heavenly home. They came in faith, and we must 'live by faith.' They were courageous, and we too must be brave if we would win our crowns.

Second Point.

'And King Herod, hearing this, was troubled, and all Jerusalem with him' (St. Matt. ii.).

It is easy to trouble those who have no trust in God. And what a strange cause for trouble—because it was hoped that the Messias, the 'King and Law-giver,' the 'Expected of the nations,' had at length come to save His people!

Third Point.

'He was in the world, and the world knew Him not' (St. John i.).

These words are true even to this day. Our Lord is in the world—first by His omnipresence as God, and then in His sacramental Presence—and great multitudes of people know Him not.

And we, the children of the Church, are we not often most irreverent and forgetful in His Presence? We know Him, it is true, but we forget Him. Let it be so no more.

January 8.

THE PROPHECIES CONCERNING THE BIRTHPLACE OF CHRIST.

First Prelude.—Imagine you see the palace of King Herod.

Second Prelude.—'Show me, O Lord, the way that leadeth unto Thee.'

First Point.

'And assembling together all the chief priests and the scribes of the people, he inquired of them where Christ should be born' (St. Matt. ii.).

The wonderful providence of God thus brought about that the prophecies concerning the Messias should be examined and read again at the very time of their fulfilment.

That same wise and loving Providence is ever watching over us, and making, as St. Paul says, 'all things work together unto good to them that love God' (Romans viii.).

So, whatever may happen to us, we are always safe.

Second Point.

'But they said to him, In Bethlehem of Juda' (St. Matt. ii.).

The Wise Men were not cast down because the star had disappeared. They persevered in their efforts to discover the Christ.

We should never be discouraged in doing what is right; and if in doubt let us seek advice from those over us. Let us go fearlessly on and follow our Lord.

Third Point.

'Then Herod, privately calling the Wise Men, learned diligently of them the time of the star which appeared to them; and, sending them into Bethlehem, said, Go and diligently inquire after the Child' (St. Matt. ii.).

Herod did not really believe the prophecies, yet he was afraid of them. He thought he had found out a sure way of securing himself without any trouble. He was trying to dupe the strangers who had come to him for information, and he was duping himself.

'The joy of the hypocrite is but for a moment' (Job xx.).

Let us always hold in horror all double-dealing and hypocrisy.

January 9.

THE THREE KINGS AT BETHLEHEM.

First Prelude.—Imagine you see the road to Bethlehem.

Second Prelude.—' Send out Thy light, O Lord, and it shall lead me.'

First Point.

'Who, having heard the king, went their way' (St. Matt. ii.).

Nothing could turn them aside from their

purpose, or hinder the onward course of these truly royal souls. The city of Jerusalem was then one of the wonders of the earth; but they turned away and went towards Bethlehem, a small obscure town.

If we want to find Jesus Christ we must turn aside from this world, and seek Him hidden in His tabernacle.

Second Point.

'And behold, the star which they had seen in the East went before them until it came and stood over where the Child was' (St. Matt. ii.).

So was their faith, their courage, their perseverance rewarded; and so when we make an effort in God's service—tell the truth, for instance, when it costs a good deal to do so, give up a companion who is doing us harm, make known to superiors something that they ought to know—we are always rewarded by inward peace, the certainty that we have done what was right.

JANUARY TENTH.

Third Point.

'And, seeing the star, they rejoiced with exceeding great joy' (St. Matt. ii.).

There is no joy like that we find in serving God, or rather there is no true joy out of Him. 'The joy of the Lord is our strength,' says the prophet (2 Esdras viii.).

The joy of the three Kings, or Wise Men, increased in proportion as they drew near Jesus Christ; and the more we see Him, and the more we prefer Him to others, the more joy we shall have; for He says Himself, by the mouth of another prophet, 'My servants shall rejoice' (Isaias lxv.).

Colloquy.—Resolution.

JANUARY 10.

THE ADORATION OF THE THREE KINGS.

First Prelude.—Imagine you see the Child in His Mother's arms, and St. Joseph with them.

Second Prelude.—' Show us at last Jesus, of thy pure womb the Fruit divine.'

First Point.

' And entering into the house, they found the Child with Mary, His Mother' (St. Matt. ii.).

Let us dwell upon these words; let us make a little silence in our hearts, and adore our dear Lord with these holy Kings.

Not only were they wise men, but they were kings, accustomed to much of Eastern splendour, and yet they saw by faith, in a little Baby in His Mother's arms, the King of kings, the Lord of hosts.

Second Point.

' And, falling down, they adored Him' (St. Matt. ii.).

What joy must have filled the hearts of our Lady and St. Joseph when they saw Him who had been born in the stable, for whom in all Bethlehem there had been no room, receive the homage of His creatures, when they saw the old prophecies fulfilled!

'The Gentiles shall walk in Thy light, and kings in the brightness of Thy rising' (Isaias lx.).

Third Point.

Let us adore Him in union with these Eastern Kings, these men who were so truly wise.

They thanked Him for having come to be the 'Light of the Gentiles' (Isaias xlii.).

Let us also thank Him that we possess the true faith, and we also walk in the 'brightness of His rising.'

They offered Him the service of their whole lives; let us also offer ourselves, 'doing the will of God from the heart, with a good will serving' (Ephesians vi.).

Colloquy.—Resolution.

January 11.

THE GIFTS OF THE THREE KINGS.

First Prelude.—Imagine you see the three Kings pouring out their gifts.

Second Prelude.—Jesus, Mary, and Joseph, I give you my heart and my soul.

First Point.

'And, opening their treasures, they offered Him gifts, gold, frankincense, and myrrh' (St. Matt. ii.).

They gave Him of all they had, whatever they counted most precious. These three gifts have many significations: first, the gold was the meet offering for a king; the frankincense, or incense, was a recognition of His Divinity; the myrrh, with which the dead are embalmed, signified that He had taken on our human nature, and should pass through the gates of death.

Second Point.

Another interpretation is that gold signified charity, incense sacrifice, and myrrh mortification.

The Saints have also loved to compare these three gifts of the three Kings to the three vows of religion : the gold that is renounced by the vow of poverty ; the myrrh of detachment, signified by the vow of chastity ; and the incense of that perfect obedience by which the religious makes himself or herself a holocaust to the Lord.

Third Point.

And there is yet another signification, a threefold offering that all of us can make : our bodies, our minds, our hearts.

We can give the body to God by carefully guarding its purity, and by using it in God's service; the mind, by thinking of God and studying how to please Him, by using the powers of our minds for His glory ; the heart, by loving Him above all things, so that we would never commit the least wilful

January 12.

THE RETURN OF THE THREE KINGS.

First Prelude.—Imagine you see the three Kings taking leave of the Child and His Mother.

Second Prelude.—' Show me Thy ways, O Lord, and teach me Thy paths.'

First Point.

' And having received an answer in sleep that they should not return to Herod, they went back another way into their country' (St. Matt. ii.).

They had then made their offering, they had spread their precious gifts at the feet of the Divine Child:

> ' To God made man, born Israel's King,
> Frankincense, myrrh, and gold they bring.'

They had spent some time in the company of of Jesus, of Mary, and of Joseph. They knew that in very truth the prophecy of Balaam was fulfilled, ' A star shall rise out of Jacob, and a sceptre shall spring up from Israel' (Numbers xxiv.); and they had seen Him who is Himself the 'bright and morning Star' (Apoc. xxii.).

Second Point.

'And having received an answer in sleep that they should not return to Herod' (St. Matt. ii.).

St. Jerome remarks that 'they who had presented unto the Lord gifts were honoured by receiving a warning, not from an angel, but from God Himself, whereas even Joseph was warned only by an angel.'

This should make us reflect on the way in which God rewards all that is done for Him, and also the care He takes of us.

Third Point.

'They went back another way into their country' (St. Matt. ii.).

St. Ambrose says, 'The Wise Men came by one way and departed by another. They that had seen Christ knew Christ, and they departed better than they came.'

They did not go back to Jerusalem to triumph over King Herod, but returned humbly to their own country.

Are we the better after we have been near our Lord in Holy Mass or at Holy Communion?

Colloquy.—Resolution.

JANUARY 13.

HOW WE SHOULD IMITATE THE WISE MEN.

First Prelude.—Imagine you see the three Kings and their train travelling homeward.

Second Prelude.—Make me to follow Thee, O Lord, in the way that Thou shalt choose.

First Point.

The Wise Men had literally done that which later on our Lord taught us all to do: 'Ask, and it shall be given unto you' (St.

They had at the peril of their lives come to Jerusalem, asking, 'Where is the King of the Jews?' and they had found Him, seen Him, adored Him.

Let us also pray in faith; be sure that God never rejects an humble earnest prayer.

Second Point.

The Wise Men had persevered against difficulties. How often do we set out with a good resolution, made, perhaps, at our meditation, or after Holy Communion, or after confession, and a little difficulty comes and all is upset! Some one laughs at us, or the carrying out of our resolve costs a little sacrifice; we get afraid.

'The slothful man saith, There is a lion without; I shall be slain in the midst of the streets' (Prov. xxii.).

Third Point.

Often have we, if we would serve God, to go back into our country by another way. God's light comes into our souls, and we see what our duty is. We can no longer be as we were before we saw it. The Wise Men had to go away from Bethlehem, though they longed to stay there:

'One little sight of Jesus was enough for many
    years;
One look at Him their stay and staff in the dismal
    vale of tears.
Their people for the sight of Him they gallantly
    withstood,
They taught His faith, they preached His word,
    and for Him shed their blood.'°

The Wise Men became martyrs, and their relics are now in the cathedral at Cologne; so let us end by invoking their help:

'Let us ask these martyrs, then, these monarchs of
    the East,
Who are sitting now in heaven at their Saviour's
    endless Feast,
To get us faith from Jesus, and hereafter faith's
    bright home,
And day and night to thank Him for the glorious
    faith of Rome.'

Colloquy.—Resolution.

° Father Faber.

January 14.

OUR LORD'S FIRST VISIT TO JERUSALEM.

First Prelude.—Imagine you see Jesus in His Mother's arms on the way to Jerusalem.

Second Prelude.—Teach me to follow Thee, O Lord, in the path Thou dost choose.

First Point.

'And after the days of her purification, they carried Him to Jerusalem' (St. Luke ii.). Let us consider each of the three persons. They were not going to travel like the three Kings, with a long train and many camels. They were very poor. Our Lady would ride on the ass, wrapping her Child up in her mantle, and St. Joseph would walk by her side.

Second Point.

Would they complain? No. Would they talk a great deal? No. Sometimes they would break out into praises of God in those psalms which were so familiar to them: 'I will pay my vows unto the Lord in the sight of all His people ; in the courts of the house of the Lord, in the midst of thee, O Jerusalem' (Ps. cxv.).

Third Point.

We have been thinking of the three Eastern Kings: how they came to Jerusalem to seek the new-born King, and ' all the city was troubled;' and now that very new-born King comes Himself, and no one is disturbed. Who would have taken notice of them? A poor man, stained with the dust of travel, leading an ass ; and a young girl, poorly clad, carrying an Infant six weeks old.

Learn to love poverty and to be unknown, after the example of Jesus, Mary, and Joseph.

Colloquy.—Resolution.

January 15.

FEAST OF ST. PAUL, THE FIRST HERMIT.

First Prelude.—Imagine you see the desert and the hermit's cell.

Second Prelude.—Make me, O Lord, to love Thee above all things.

First Point.

Towards the middle of the third century a young Christian retired into the desert, and took up his abode in a cave. There he lived nearly one hundred years. As time went on many followed his example and became hermits. A hermit means a person who lives in entire solitude with God. Only those specially called by God can follow this life; and the Church holds all hermits in great veneration.

'O all ye holy monks and hermits,' she prays in the Litanies of the Saints; and when a soul is passing from earth, she bids it depart 'in the name of the holy monks and hermits' (Ritual).

Second Point.

Near the cave where St. Paul lived was a palm-tree, and its fruit served him for food and its leaves for clothing. And besides this every day a raven brought him half a loaf of bread.

St. Anthony the Abbot was told by God to go and see St. Paul. On that day the raven brought a whole loaf.

'Well,' quoth St. Paul, 'the Lord hath sent us our dinner. Truly He is gracious, truly He is merciful. It is now sixty years that I have had half a loaf of bread every day; but now that thou art come Christ giveth His soldiers double rations.'

Do we thank God for any unexpected blessing?

Third Point.

Soon after this St. Paul died, and St. Anthony saw his soul ascending to heaven amidst choirs of Angels, Prophets, and Apostles. St. Anthony did not know how he should dig a grave for his holy friend, as he had no spade, when he saw two lions racing towards him, as though to assist at the burial; and they scratched a hole big enough for a man's grave with their paws.

We ought to hold in great reverence all those who live a life of prayer and penance; and even though very far off, we ought to copy them by the little acts of mortification that are in our power.

Colloquy.—Resolution.

January 16.

JESUS IS PRESENTED IN THE TEMPLE.

First Prelude.—Imagine you see the inside of the beautiful temple of Jerusalem.

Second Prelude.—Grant, O Lord, I may be presented unto Thee with a pure and clean heart.

JANUARY SIXTEENTH.

First Point.

'His parents brought in the Child Jesus, to do for Him according to the custom of the law' (St. Luke ii.).

The prophet Malachias had spoken of the coming of the Lord to His temple, and he had said, 'Who shall be able to think of the day of His coming, and who shall stand to see Him?' (Malachias iii.)

Very different was this His first coming: a little Infant lying in His Mother's arms!

Imagine the great temple, with its many courts and doors, and the crowds going in and out, and no one noticing the Mother and the Child. Yet He was the Creator of all things, and she was the Immaculate one.

Second Point.

The first temple at Jerusalem was built by King Solomon about a thousand years before the birth of our Lord; its beauty and magnificence made it a marvel in the earth; but as a punishment to the Jews it was destroyed after about four hundred years. It was rebuilt later, though very far short of its former magnificence, so that those who saw this house in its first glory found this in comparison as nothing (Aggeus ii.); but when our Lady entered with her Child, she might have said, 'There is here One greater than the temple' (St. Matt. xii.). It is God's grace that gives true beauty.

Third Point.

God, speaking by His Prophets, had made great promises concerning this second temple, and now the day of their fulfilment had come. He had said, 'The Desired of all nations shall come, and I will fill this house with glory' (Aggeus ii.). Yet still the Jews were ignorant that the word of the Lord was this day kept before them.

Let us be afraid of missing any inspiration or light from God by not listening to His voice when He speaks to us through our superiors.

January 17.

JESUS IS REDEEMED ACCORDING TO THE LAW.

First Prelude. — Imagine you see St. Joseph carrying two little doves into the temple.

Second Prelude.—Help me, Thy servant, whom Thou hast redeemed with Thy Precious Blood.

First Point.

' And to offer a sacrifice according as it is written in the law of the Lord: a pair of turtle doves, or two young pigeons' (St. Luke ii.).

These words at once reveal that Mary and Joseph were among the poor; for the law said that a lamb was to be the offering; ' but if she is not able to offer the lamb, she shall take two turtles or two young pigeons.' What a wonderful pattern of humility is here set before us! Our Lady and our Lord willingly reckoning themselves among the poor!

How it ought to teach us a contempt for

riches, since we see that our Lord would never touch them! He was born in poverty, and in it He would live and die.

Second Point.

'But if she is not able to offer the lamb' (Leviticus xii.).

Yet surely no mother on the earth was ever more able to offer the lamb; for was not her Beloved Child Himself the 'Lamb of God, who taketh away the sin of the world'? (St. John i.)

It was the beginning of the great sacrifice, to last not only to Calvary but beyond, 'even to the consummation of the world' (St. Matt. xxviii.).

He offered Himself once by His Mother's hands in the Jewish temple; but on our altars He offers Himself 'from the rising of the sun even to the going down' (Malachias i.).

Third Point.

Very obediently did Mary and Joseph obey

the letter of the law, and bring their Precious Child to the 'door of the tabernacle of the testimony;' and very humbly did they kneel while the priest offered the Child and the doves to the Lord and prayed for His Mother.

What a lesson we should learn here of obedience to rules and customs and wishes of superiors! Sometimes these rules seem to us tiresome and useless, and we count the transgression of them a little thing; yet all and each are an expression to us of God's will for us.

Colloquy.—Resolution.

January 18.

Feast of St. Peter's Chair in Rome.

First Prelude.—Imagine you see St. Peter saying Mass in secret in pagan Rome.

Second Prelude.—Hail, Rome, Eternal Citadel, whence our faith has sprung!

First Point.

St. Peter became the first Bishop of Rome, and like a humble pilgrim the Prince of the Apostles entered the Imperial City. Pope St. Leo says that every error was gathered together in Rome, and here it was St. Peter came to set up the standard of truth. He had founded already the see of Antioch, he had preached the Gospel in many countries, and in his old age he came to Rome. What an example does this set us of persevering love for God!

Second Point.

St. Peter had of course to hide himself in Rome. One house where he often lived was that of the Senator Pudens, who, with his wife and two daughters, were among the early converts of the Saint.

On the site of this house a church was afterwards built, dedicated to St. Pudenziana, one of the daughters of Pudens, who won the crown of martyrdom. There may still be seen the altar on which St. Peter said Mass.

What great love and veneration we should have for the first Pope, he to whom was committed by our Lord Himself 'the keys of the kingdom of heaven'! How firmly should we cling to our faith!

Third Point.

Rome is built on seven hills. On one of them, the Aventine, was the house of St. Prisca, a noble Roman maiden, whom St. Peter likewise baptised. The font is still preserved, and here he also baptised Aquila and Priscilla. St. Prisca was martyred, after cruel torments, at the age of thirteen.

Thus did St. Peter plant the Church of God in Rome; and God chose this city for His own, to be the earthly type of the Heavenly Jerusalem. So we ought to love it, and to grieve deeply whenever the evil hands of lawless men despoil and oppress the Eternal City.

January 19.

HOLY SIMEON.

First Prelude.—Imagine you see the temple in Jerusalem, as before.

Second Prelude.—Show to me, sweet Mother, the fruit of thy womb, Jesus.

First Point.

'And he had received an answer from the Holy Ghost that he should not see death before he had seen the Christ of the Lord' (St. Luke ii.).

Holy Simeon is the type of patient waiting, of long-continued prayer, of rooted confidence in God. How often we are impatient if our prayers are not heard directly we make them! If we are not able to carry out our resolutions and plans at once, how soon we lose heart and give up! But God loves patience and perseverance.

The Psalms of David are full of words like these: 'Wait on the Lord' (Ps. xxxvii.);

and the prophet Isaias says, 'I will wait for the Lord' (Isaias viii.).

Second Point.

'He also took Him into his arms and blessed God' (St. Luke ii.)

Let us contemplate this wonderful picture: the old man on the brink of the grave, the Infant of a few weeks. 'The old man held his Lord in his arms in the form of a little child, but the Child was the old man's King.'*

Third Point.

'And said, Now Thou dost dismiss Thy servant, O Lord, according to Thy word, in peace. Because my eyes have seen Thy salvation' (St. Luke ii.).

And so again was the prophecy fulfilled: 'Great shall be the glory of this house, more than that of the first, saith the Lord of hosts; and in this place I will give peace, saith the Lord of hosts' (Aggeus ii.).

° Ant. for Vespers.

JANUARY TWENTIETH.

Those who serve the Lord always have peace of soul. They may have to suffer much, and to give up many things, but they need never lose their peace. We all know the peace that follows when we obey the voice of our conscience, when we have made a good confession. Let us try never, then, to lose this precious gift.

Colloquy.—Resolution.

JANUARY 20.

FEAST OF SS. FABIAN AND SEBASTIAN.

First Prelude.—Imagine you see the courtyard and the post erected.

Second Prelude.—O patient St. Sebastian, aid me in the strife with temptation.

First Point.

St. Sebastian was a Roman soldier, and a great favourite with the Emperor Diocletian, who made him captain of the Prætorian Guards. When the Emperor found out that Sebastian was a Christian, he was furious, and ordered him to be tied to a post and shot to death with arrows. There are times in our lives when arrows are shot at us, the arrows of the devil's temptations—'The arrow that flieth in the day' (Ps. xc.)—and cruel and false words may be said against us, 'False witness is like a sharp arrow' (Prov. xxv.).

Even children have to meet with these arrows at times; let us look at the noble St. Sebastian, and take courage.

Second Point.

St. Sebastian was left for dead; but when the Christians took away the body to bury it, they found him alive. He was taken care of, and recovered. Undaunted he went before the Emperor to reprove him for his crimes. He was then beaten with rods till he gave up his soul to God. He endured all this; and cannot we bear a little suffering for our Lord's sake? What matter if people scoff and sneer at our holy faith; let us love it all the more, and be ready, if need be, to die for it.

Third Point.

The body of St. Sebastian was buried in one of the Catacombs, which was afterwards known by his name. Later on a church was built as a resting-place for his body, and it became one of the seven Basilicas of Rome. In it there is a beautiful marble statue of the Saint pierced with arrows; and among the treasures of this church is one of the arrows that was buried in his flesh.

St. Sebastian is regarded as one of the special protectors of the Church. Let us invoke him, then, with great confidence to obtain for us a deep spirit of devotion and fidelity to our Holy Mother the Church.

Colloquy.—Resolution.

January 21.

FEAST OF ST. AGNES.

First Prelude. — Imagine you see the court and the cruel judges.

Second Prelude.—Blessed St. Agnes, now glorious in heaven, help me.

First Point.

One of the special glories of St. Agnes is that she is patroness of the young; and it shows how holy children should be, since the most spotless Saints are chosen as their patrons, and no child can say, after having heard the story of St. Agnes, that he or she is too young to serve God well. She was but thirteen. St. Ambrose says: ' She overcame the weakness of childhood, and witnessed a good confession. Her little body was hardly big enough to give play to the instruments of their cruelty; but if they could scarce sheathe their swords in her slight frame, they found in her that which laughed the power of the sword to scorn.' Shall I, then, be conquered by a foolish word or a base temptation?

Second Point.

St. Agnes is ever regarded as a model of angelical purity, and this she united to the most ardent love for Jesus Christ. She said, 'I keep my troth to Him alone, at whose beauty the sun and moon do wonder.' If we love God, and desire to see His Face, we must jealously guard the treasure of innocence given to us in Holy Baptism.

Third Point.

The Church on this day, in her offices, puts these words into the mouth of holy Agnes: 'Rejoice with me, and make merry, because I also have secured a throne in light. Christ hath crowned me with the bright and priceless blossoms of the eternal springtime.' And then the Church continues: 'Let us keep with joy and gladness the feast of this most saintly maiden; let us call to mind the holy passion of the Blessed Agnes; in her thirteenth year she conquered, losing death and finding life, because she loved the only Giver of life.'

Let us, then, rejoice on this holy feast, choose St. Agnes as a special patron, and ask her to teach us how to imitate her.

Colloquy.—Resolution.

January 22.

THE PROPHECY OF SIMEON.

First Prelude.—Imagine you see the temple as on previous occasions.

Second Prelude.—

'O thou Mother, fount of love!
Touch my spirit from above,
Let my heart with thine accord.'

First Point.

'And Simeon blessed them, and said to

JANUARY TWENTY-SECOND.

Mary, His Mother, Behold, this Child is set for the fall and for the resurrection of many in Israel, and for a sign which shall be contradicted' (St. Luke ii.).

We too often forget the truth that the service of God is a warfare: we often resolve to be good, and then, when a difficulty comes, we give up the struggle. We will do what is right when it is easy, but not when it costs us anything.

Let us learn that when the will of God, as revealed to us by our conscience or by orders given to us, is in *contradiction* to our own desires, we must yield instantly with perfect submission.

Second Point.

'And thy own soul a sword shall pierce' (St. Luke ii.).

Earthly joy is very transitory, for this world is not the place for joy. Our good God often gives us some of it from time to of joy; but even while they have it their souls should be trained to meet the sorrows and cares of after life.

Into the midst of Mary's joy came the words of Simeon, reminding her that, as she was the Mother of God, she must be also the Mother of Sorrows; for He came on earth to suffer and to redeem, and she, who was so closely knit together with Him, must suffer also.

If, then, we never bear the cross, we can never, as St. Peter says, 'partake of the sufferings of Christ,' and therefore not be able to 'rejoice when His glory shall be revealed' (1 St. Peter iv.).

Third Point.

The peculiar suffering of our Lady from the prophecy which the Church calls the first of her Seven Dolours, can hardly be understood by the young. It gave her the sorrow of suspense, the dread of the future, the constant apprehension of losing Him who was to her more than life. 'When a carpenter's tool pressed against the palm of His hand, she saw the wound of the nail there. The white brow of boyhood often seemed as if it had a coronal of rosy spots around where the thorns should be.'*

If we cannot understand this first dolour of our Mother, let us love her all the more for having borne it for our sakes.

Colloquy.—Resolution.

January 23.

ESPOUSALS OF OUR LADY.

First Prelude.—Imagine you see the temple and the High-Priest.

Second Prelude.—O Holy Virgin Mary, grant that all who keep thy holy bridal-feast may feel the might of thine assistance.

First Point.

' A Virgin espoused to a man whose name

* Father Faber, *Foot of the Cross.*

was Joseph, of the house of David; and the Virgin's name was Mary' (St. Luke i.).

Both Mary and Joseph belonged to the tribe of David, the royal line of the kings of Juda; for God had promised this to David, the 'man according to His own heart' (1 Kings xiii.), and thus our Lord was constantly called the Son of David. The first chapter of the Gospel of St. Matthew traces the descent of our Lord from David, and through him from Abraham, and thus the promise to Abraham was fulfilled: 'And in thy seed shall all the nations of the earth be blessed, because thou hast obeyed My voice' (Gen. xxii.).

When we see how God fulfilled the promises He had made to the patriarchs, it ought to fill our hearts with loving trust in Him.

Second Point.

Our Lady had spent twelve years in the temple, and she was now espoused by the

High-Priest to Joseph, whom the Holy Ghost says was a 'just man.' Our Lady then left the temple for Nazareth, for the house where tradition says she had been born, and which she now gave to St. Joseph as her marriage dowry. What a happy lot was that of St. Joseph to be. chosen to be the spouse and protector of Mary, and the witness of the Incarnation!

Let us try to increase our love and devotion to this glorious Saint.

Third Point.

The Church is full of joy on this feast. She says in her Office, ' Let us this day keep solemnly the bridal-feast of Mary, Mother, but still Maiden, her bridal a step towards the loftiness of her throne;' and again she says, 'Thy betrothal, O Virgin Mother of God, was a message of joy to the whole world.' Let us, then, rejoice with our dearest Mother on this day of joy to her, for then she received from God a great gift, a faithful friend. The wise King Solomon says, 'Who shall find a faithful man?' (Prov. xx.) And again he says, 'He that is a friend loveth at all times' (Prov. xvii.). Such was St. Joseph, the spouse of Mary, truly faithful, truly self-forgetting. Let us, then, please our Lady by loving Him who so dearly loved her.

Colloquy.—Resolution.

JANUARY 24.

THE PROPHETESS ANNA.

First Prelude.—Imagine you see the temple, in which she served so long.

Second Prelude.—Let Thy mercy, O Lord, be my comfort.

First Point.

'And there was one Anna, a prophetess, the daughter of Phanuel, of the tribe of Aser. She was far advanced in years. And she was a widow until fourscore and four years, who departed not from the temple, by fastings and prayers serving night and day' (St. Luke ii.).

There were three women who bore the name of Anna who were all favoured by God: the first was the mother of Samuel the prophet, of whom it is said she 'multiplied prayers before the Lord' (1 Kings i.); the second was the holy Anna of the temple; and the third that happy and glorious St. Anna, the Mother of our Lady. All these three holy women were remarkable for their spirit of prayer.

Let us try, then, to pray often, to pray earnestly and in faith.

Second Point.

' Now she at the same time coming in, confessed to the Lord' (St. Luke ii.). Here was another answer to prayer, another proof how pleasing mortification is to God, what blessings it draws from Him. Again we see how Anna's constant dwelling in the temple was rewarded. If we stay in the place where God calls us, we shall receive the grace He intends for us; but if we are not there, if we prefer to go our own way, thinking that obedience to a call or a signal is tiresome and to be avoided, then we shall miss it, as Anna would if she had not come in 'at the same time.'

Third Point.

'And spoke of Him to all that looked for the redemption of Israel' (St. Luke ii.).

Those who love our Lord always want to bring others to Him. If we are united to Him we catch a spark of that zeal which consumed Him. Even children can be in their way apostles; not by setting themselves up above their superiors, but by their good example, by their courage. The child who speaks the truth, the child who will report to superiors that which they ought to know, trampling under foot ridicule and dislike, is helping our Lord.

Let us, then, try and do all we can to help our companions on the road to heaven.
Colloquy.—Resolution.

January 25.

CONVERSION OF ST. PAUL THE APOSTLE.

First Prelude.—Imagine you see the great gates of the city of Damascus, where St. Paul had arrived.

Second Prelude.—Lead us, great teacher Paul, in wisdom's ways, and lift our hearts with thine to Heaven's high throne.

First Point.

'And Saul was still breathing out threatenings and slaughter against the disciples of the Lord; and as he went on his journey suddenly there shined round about him a light from heaven. And he fell to the earth, and heard a voice saying unto him, Saul, Saul, why persecutest thou Me? And he said,

JANUARY TWENTY-FIFTH.

Who art Thou, Lord? And the Lord said, I am Jesus, whom thou persecutest' (Acts ix.).

Saul had been full of false zeal against the Church; he had consented to the death of St. Stephen; but that Saint had prayed for his murderers, and here was the answer to his prayer. Our Lord spoke to Saul from heaven, and his heart was instantly changed.

Every day our dear Lord is working miracles of grace in the hearts of His people, calling some from the darkness of error to the light of truth, some from the service of His enemies to be His faithful soldiers.

Are we acting up to the graces He gives to us?

Second Point.

'And he, trembling and astonished, said, Lord, what wilt Thou have me to do? And the Lord said unto him, Arise, and go into the city, and it shall there be told thee what thou must do' (Acts ix.).

St. Paul was converted by our Lord's own voice and by miracle, and then he was told to go and submit himself like a child to the guide whom God would give him.

What a lesson we have here of submission to the Church, to our confessors and spiritual directors! Our Lord was teaching St. Paul the lesson, 'Unless you be converted and become as little children, you shall not enter into the kingdom of heaven.' If children are set thus as an example to their elders, what ought they themselves to be? What must our Lord think of a proud obstinate child that will not be taught?

Third Point.

'This man is to Me a vessel of election, to carry My name before the Gentiles and kings and the children of Israel' (Acts ix.).

St. Paul was called to be great in the kingdom of God; therefore he was first brought low and 'humbled under the mighty hand of God' (1 Peter v.).

St. Peter had learnt humility by his fall; and St. Paul, so full of pride, was 'led by the hand into Damascus,' and was 'there three days without sight, and he did neither eat nor drink.' He afterwards became the great pillar of the Church, holding the place next to St. Peter. The Church celebrates their memory on one feast, and their sacred heads are side by side in the Basilica of St. John Lateran at Rome.

Let us ask this Saint to obtain for us an ardent love for Jesus Christ.

Colloquy.—Resolution.

January 26.

THE RETURN TO NAZARETH.

First Prelude.—Imagine the road (of about eighty miles) between Jerusalem and Nazareth.

Second Prelude.—O my God, make haste to help me.

First Point.

There is a well-founded tradition that, after the Presentation in the Temple, the Holy Family returned home. They were not likely to linger in Jerusalem; they loved to be obscure and unknown.

If we want to find our Lord and to be near to Him, we must be humble, modest, and retired. There is no other way. Am I walking in it?

Second Point.

Tradition also says the Holy Family on their way to Nazareth stopped to rest at the house of St. Anne. Our Lady, who fondly loved her father and mother, was sure to wish to show them her Child. What must have been the rapture of St. Joachim and St. Anne when they saw the Child Jesus, and when they learned that He was indeed the Messias, and that their beloved daughter was indeed the happy being spoken of in prophecies—the woman of whom God, speaking to the Evil One, said, 'She shall crush thy head' (Genesis iii.).

Let us rejoice with St. Joachim and St. Anne in the glory of our Lady.

Third Point.

Imagine with what joy and gratitude Mary and Joseph must have reëntered their home at Nazareth, bearing with them their Treasure. How they must have adored and prayed to God! With what earnestness they asked God to give them light and grace to fulfil the wonderful charge He had confided to them!

Do I seek God's help in my difficulties? When what I have to do seems beyond my strength am I certain that I 'can do all things in Him who strengtheneth me'? (Phil. iv.)

Colloquy.—Resolution.

January 27.

CHILDHOOD OF ST. JOHN THE BAPTIST.

First Prelude.—Imagine you see the sandy desert and its solitude.

Second Prelude.—Dear Lord, make me fear nothing, save to offend Thee.

First Point.

'And the child grew and was strengthened in spirit, and was in the deserts until the day of his manifestation to Israel' (St. Luke i.).

There is a constant tradition that our Lord and St. John the Baptist were together in their infancy, and artists have loved to paint the scene. This must have been the time they were together, before the flight into Egypt. We can well imagine how St. Elizabeth would love to sit by our Lady's side, and gaze upon her and the Divine Child, saying often in her heart, 'Whence is this to me, that I should be in the company of the Mother of my Lord?' and we can imagine the Divine Child and the little John playing together at their mothers' feet.

Second Point.

At a very early age St. John went into the desert. This seems a fearful thing for a little child, but St. John was not like other children. He was sanctified before his birth. Mary, bearing within her the Incarnate God, was present at his birth; and St. Ambrose says, 'We know nothing of his childhood, but we know it was safe and strong through the nearness of the Lord.'

If we want to be safe and delivered from fear we must keep close to Jesus and Mary, and if we avoid sin we can dwell in their company.

Third Point.

'The same John had his garment of camel's hair, and a leathern girdle about his loins, and his meat was locusts and wild honey' (St. Matt. iii.).

JANUARY TWENTY-SEVENTH.

St. John the Baptist is a type of innocence and also a type of penance, and other youthful Saints have followed in the same road.

The innocent love God; they are near to Him.

'Blessed are the clean of heart, for they shall see God' (St. Matt. v.).

Then those who see Him become like to Him, and are filled with burning zeal, and they do penance. The slightest blemish in themselves is far more dreadful in their eyes than grave sins are to us; and then they yearn to make reparation for the injuries done to God by sin, and to do penance for those who will not do penance for themselves.

Seeing this wonderful pattern of innocence and penance, let us be faithful in our acts of mortification.

Colloquy.—Resolution.

January 28.

OCTAVE OF ST. AGNES.

First Prelude.—Imagine you see St. Agnes in glory.

Second Prelude.—Blessed St. Agnes, teach me to follow thee.

First Point.

'Emerentiana was a Roman maiden, and the foster-sister of the Blessed Agnes. While still only a catechumen she was stoned to death, and was only able to drag herself to the grave of holy Agnes, where she gave up her soul, being baptised, not in water, but in her own blood, so freely shed for Christ.'*

A catechumen means a person under instruction for Holy Baptism. Here are the first-fruits of the good confession for Christ made by St. Agnes. She won for her foster-sister the crown of martyrdom.

Let us try and obtain some good gift by her intercession.

º Roman Breviary.

Second Point.

'One night, when the parents of the Blessed Agnes were watching at her grave, she appeared to them in company with a band of Virgins, and said to them, "Father and mother, weep not for me as though I were dead; for now these Virgins and I live together in Him, whose love was my whole life on earth."'*

What joy must then have filled her parents' hearts!

Let us also rejoice and have great confidence in our sweet Patron Saint, knowing she can obtain great things from Him in 'whom she lives.'

Third Point.

'Some years afterwards, Constance, the daughter of the Emperor Constantine, being sick of an incurable ulcer, betook herself to the said grave, although she was not yet a Christian; and as she lay by it and slept she

* Roman Breviary.

seemed to hear the voice of Agnes saying to her, "Constance, be of good courage; believe in Jesus Christ the Son of God, and He will make thee whole."

'The princess, being healed, was baptised.'*

Constance afterwards built a church over the burial-place of St. Agnes. It is a most lovely one, and there, to this day, the Virgin Saint reposes. Constance is herself reckoned among the Saints; and a church in her honour stands hard by the Basilica of St. Agnes.

Each of us may now hear the 'voice of Agnes.' To each of us she says, 'Be of good courage; believe in Jesus Christ.'

If we had lively faith we could become Saints. Let us, then, pray earnestly, 'Lord, increase my faith.'

Colloquy.—Resolution.

° Roman Breviary.

January 29.

FEAST OF ST. FRANCIS OF SALES.

First Prelude.—Imagine you see the Saint, as a child, kneeling by his mother's side.

Second Prelude.—Teach me, dear Saint, ever to be gentle and reverent and truthful.

First Point.

St. Francis of Sales was holy in his childhood.

Two virtues specially were remarked in him as a child, his reverence in church and his truthfulness.

The writer of his life says, 'In the church he used to kneel by his mother's side, his hands clasped, his eyes fixed on the altar; and his whole manner was so reverent, he seemed like an angel.'

What about my conduct in church? Do I kneel in a reverent manner? or do I stare about?

In every sanctuary there are angels prostrate in adoration : am I trying to join with them?

Second Point.

It is recorded of St. Francis that no one ever knew him to tell the smallest falsehood, or to try in any way to deceive, and he would rather suffer punishment than tell a lie.

Once he was punished severely because he had courage to own his fault. Do I cultivate this great virtue of truth? Our Lady says to us, 'A mouth with a double tongue do I hate' (Prov. viii.). Our Lord said, speaking of the devil, 'He is a liar, and the father thereof' (St. John viii.).

Let us therefore try to be simple and truthful in word and deed.

Third Point.

St. Francis, in his childhood, was distinguished by his love for the poor. His joy was to help them. Whenever he was allowed he would give them part of his dinner, and if he saw them sent away without relief his tears used to flow.

Do I try to help the poor, even if it be in a very slight way?

It is not the amount we give to others that God values, but the self-denial it costs us.

When our Lord saw a poor widow cast into the treasury of the temple one farthing, He said she had given the most of all, 'For they did cast in of their abundance; but she, of her want, cast in all she had' (St. Matt. xii.).

Colloquy.—Resolution.

January 30.

ST. MARTINA, VIRGIN AND MARTYR.

First Prelude.—Imagine you see the wild beasts in the Colosseum in Rome.

Second Prelude.—Blessed Saint, gain for me courage to follow our Lord.

JANUARY THIRTIETH.

First Point.

St. Martina was a young Roman maiden of very noble birth. She gave all her fortune to the poor. As she refused to sacrifice to idols, she was cruelly tortured and scourged by iron prongs and hooks.

How often are we angry when we receive a punishment even when we have deserved it! Yet this young noble girl thought nothing of the cruel scourging she endured for love of Him who Himself was scourged for love of us.

Second Point.

Then Martina was carried to the Colosseum in Rome, which is built in the form of an amphitheatre, so that spectators sitting on raised seats could see what was going on in the middle space on the ground. Wild beasts were let loose, and then this marvel took place:

'In vain they cast her to the ravenous beasts;
Calm at her feet the lion crouches down.'°

° Father Caswall's translations.

This is by no means the only instance in the lives of the martyrs where the wild beasts refused to touch them; for it is true of them as it was of their King: 'Thou shouldest not have any power against Me unless it were given thee from above' (St. John xix.).

Third Point.

Then Martina was cast into the fire, but it did not hurt her. 'She lay praying with a brightness in her face, while a matter like milk oozed from her body along with the blood, emitting a soft sweet smell.'*

Many of the spectators were converted, and, confessing Christ, were martyred in their turn; and when at last the head of the virgin was severed from the body a peal louder than thunder shook the city, and 'seemed as a voice to call her home.' She was ever held in great veneration in Rome.

Let us invoke her now, and ask her to pray for the Eternal City:

'Plead maiden for thy native land,
Plead for thy Mother Church of Rome.
o o o o o
Rome calls upon thee, that the prayers,
Not rising from one shore alone,
May from thy odour-phial float
Towards the Everlasting Throne.'o

Colloquy.—Resolution.

January 31.

THE HOLY NAME OF JESUS.

First Prelude.—Imagine you see the Angel saying to our Lady, 'Thou shalt call His Name Jesus.'

Second Prelude.—Make me, O Lord, to have a perpetual fear and love of Thy Holy Name.

First Point.

'A Name which is above every name. That in the Name of Jesus every knee should bow, of those that are in heaven, on earth, and under the earth' (Philippians ii.).

How we should love the Name of our dear Lord! how we should trust in it. Nothing that we ask in His Name will be refused: 'Whatsoever ye shall ask the Father in My Name, that will I do' (St. John xiv.).

When we want help to overcome a temptation, or strength to deny ourselves, and we feel we cannot do it, let us say, 'Lord Jesus, help me,' and we shall be victorious.

Second Point.

'His Name was called Jesus, that was called by the Angel.'

Jesus means Saviour; therefore our Lord chose it to show us He had come into the world to save and to bless. When we feel how hard it is to conquer our evil natures, to become good, let us take courage, for we serve Him whose Name is Saviour.

Third Point.

us how He longs for our salvation, to have us with Him in heaven. Let us, then, try hard to give Him what He seeks—the love of our hearts, the service of our lives.

Colloquy.—Resolution.

A.M.D.G.

MEDITATIONS FOR THE YOUNG

REVISED BY A JESUIT FATHER.

February.

LONDON: BURNS AND OATES.
DUBLIN: M. H. GILL AND SON, SACKVILLE STREET.
Price Fourpence; or Three Shillings per Dozen.

Nihil obstat.   A. DIGNAM, S.J.

Imprimatur.
                       HENRICUS EDUARDUS,
                          Card. Archiep. Westmonast.

Die 30 Nov. 1879.

HELPS TO MEDITATION.*

1. BEFORE going to bed read over the points of your meditation, and let the subject be as far as possible your last thought.
2. On rising in the morning recall the subject of your meditation.
3. Avoid talking unnecessarily till the meditation has been made.
4. Do not kneel down hastily and begin, but think seriously first that God is looking at you.
5. Begin by a little hearty act of self-humiliation, and be sure to invoke our Lady and St. Joseph.
6. Try and carry away from meditation at least one thought to recall during the day.
7. Sometimes it is useful to write down a thought that has struck you in meditation.
8. Do not let your resolutions be vague, such as, 'I will try always to be charitable;' but, 'I will

* By accident this page was omitted in the January number. It has been printed in such a manner that, if the numbers are bound into a volume at the end of the year, this page can be put in its proper place.

sion,' &c.

LENT AND EASTERTIDE.

The difficulty of arranging a meditation-book for every month which shall also include a course of meditations for Lent and Eastertide has been met in the following manner: Easter Sunday is supposed to fall on April 1st, and a series of Meditations is given from the 15th to the 30th of April, which can be used either before or after Easter, as the actual date of the feast may require.*

As February is a short month, in order to make each monthly number uniform in size, supplementary Meditations have been added for two feasts that fall in the month of March, which some may prefer to use on those days.

* Later in the year another series of Meditations will be given, which can also be used in this interval.

CONTENTS.

FEB.   PAGE

1. ST. BRIGID, VIRGIN AND PATRONESS OF IRELAND 81
2. THE PURIFICATION OF OUR LADY, OR CANDLEMAS-DAY 84
3. DREAM OF ST. JOSEPH 87
4. THE FLIGHT INTO EGYPT . . . 90
5. THE HOLY FAMILY IN EGYPT . . . 93
6. RETURN OF THE HOLY FAMILY . . 98
7. THE HOLY CHILDHOOD 101
8. GOING UP TO JERUSALEM 103
9. THE LOSS OF THE CHILD JESUS . . 106
10. OUR LADY AND ST. JOSEPH SEEK THE CHILD , ... 109
11. THE FINDING IN THE TEMPLE . . . 112
12. GOING DOWN TO NAZARETH . . . 115
13. THE HOLY HOUSE AT NAZARETH . . 118
14. THE HIDDEN LIFE 121

FEB.	PAGE
15. ASH-WEDNESDAY	125
16. THE RIGHT USE OF LENT	128
17. OUR LORD IN THE DESERT	132
18. OUR LORD TEMPTED BY THE DEVIL	135
19. THE SAME (CONTINUED)	138
20. THE ANGELS IN THE DESERT	142
21. BETHANIA	145
22. THE PALM-BRANCHES	148
23. THE TEARS OF OUR LORD	151
24. THE CHILDREN'S HOSANNA	155
25. THE BARREN FIG-TREE	158
26. THE PASCH	160
27. OUR LORD WASHES HIS DISCIPLES' FEET	164
28. THE SAME (CONTINUED)	167
29. JUDAS ISCARIOT	170

SUPPLEMENTARY MEDITATIONS
FOR THE MONTH OF MARCH.

1. FEAST OF ST. PATRICK, APOSTLE OF IRELAND	173
2. FEAST OF ST. JOSEPH, HUSBAND OF OUR LADY	175

February.

February 1.

ST. BRIGID, VIRGIN AND PATRONESS OF IRELAND.

First Prelude.—Imagine you see the rudely-built church in which the Saint made her religious profession.

Second Prelude.—O Lord, help me for the sake of Thy blessed handmaiden.

First Point.

St. Brigid, or St. Bride (as she is sometimes called), was holy in her childhood. When she was very little, her father saw, in a vision, men in white raiment pouring oil on her head, and, in the words of Holy Church: 'As soon as she had attained her first years of girlhood she chose Christ, her

Saviour, for her bridegroom, and clung to Him with so profound a passion of her heart, that she gave away to the poor whatsoever she had.'* Is God's love and service the first object of my life ? Am I always ready to give up what He asks from me ?

Second Point.

St. Brigid wished to consecrate herself to God. There were then no nuns in Ireland, so the Saint founded the religious life for women in that country.

Fearing that her extraordinary beauty might be a snare to her, she prayed our Lord to take it away. He did so; but on the day of her profession, when she had put on her white habit and bowed her head to receive the sacred veil, she touched the wooden step of the altar, and instantly the dry wood became green, and all disfigurement disappeared from her fair face. St. Brigid was willing to sacrifice beauty to gain closer

° Roman Breviary.

union with our Lord; and how often do we sin, or waste our time in trying to set ourselves off, or to look better than others!

Third Point.

St. Brigid lived at the same time as St. Patrick, and she regarded him with the deepest veneration and love. It was granted to her to stand by his bed of death, and the linen she had woven enwrapped his sacred body; and when the time came for her ' to give up her beautiful soul to her Bridegroom, Christ,' she was ' laid in the same grave with the blessed Patrick.'

Let us ask this sweet Saint to obtain for us a love of true beauty, and a great courage in doing the will of God.

Colloquy.—Resolution.

February 2.

THE PURIFICATION OF OUR LADY, OR CANDLEMAS-DAY.

First Prelude.—Imagine you see the Temple at Jerusalem.

Second Prelude.—From the fear of being humbled deliver me, Jesus.

First Point.

'After the days of her purification, according to the law of Moses, were accomplished' (St. Luke ii.).

Except our Blessed Lady and her Divine Child, all the human race are conceived and born in original sin. As a token of this the Jewish mothers could not enter the Temple for forty days after the birth of a son; and then they brought an offering and were prayed for by the priest, and this was called their purification.

Why did our Lady submit to this? Why did she not say, 'I am exempt; I am the Immaculate Virgin Mother'?

Because she was 'full of grace,' and therefore rooted and grounded in humility; for humility is the soil in which all other virtues grow, and those who are really humble never refuse, but rather seek after, humiliations.

Am I not always eager to escape blame? to maintain what I call my rights? to boast of my privileges?

Second Point.

'A light to the revelation of the Gentiles' (St. Luke ii.).

These words were spoken by holy Simeon on the day of our Lady's purification; and therefore, on this feast, the Church has instituted the beautiful custom of blessing candles, which are then held by the people, lighted during Mass, whence the name Candlemas.

Our Lord said, 'I am the light of the world' (St. John viii.). The Catholic Church enjoys the full light of God's truth. 'You are the children of the light,' says St. Paul (1 Thess. v.).

Then let us remember our two great obligations to 'walk as children of the light,' as also says St. Paul, 'For the fruit of the light is in all goodness and justice and truth' (Eph. v.); and again our Lord Himself says to us, 'You are the light of the world; let your light shine before men.' All of us, even small children, can set a good example, and thus let our light shine before men.

Third Point.

'My eyes have seen Thy salvation' (St. Luke ii.).

Candlemas-day is the end of Christmas-tide. It often falls after Septuagesima Sunday, and so the coming shadows of Lent mingle with Christmas joys. As one of our living poets has said so beautifully:

> 'The angel lights of Christmas morn,
> Which shot across the sky,
> Away they pass at Candlemas,
> They sparkle and they die.

> Comfort of earth is brief at best,
> Although it be divine ;
> Like funeral lights for Christmas gone
> Old Simeon's tapers shine.'

Christmas-tide then is over. I can say with holy Simeon, 'My eyes have seen Thy salvation.' Has it done its work in me? Has it left me more like the Infant Jesus than it found me? If we have grown more like Jesus and Mary, by keeping in their company, we can each of us say with joy:

> 'And still though Candlemas be spent,
> And Alleluias o'er,
> Mary is music in our need,
> And Jesus light in store.'°

Colloquy.—Resolution.

February 3.

DREAM OF ST. JOSEPH.

First Prelude.—Imagine you see the pallet

° Cardinal Newman.

on which St. Joseph is sleeping, an angel bending over him.

Second Prelude.—Make me, O Lord, always to do Thy most holy will.

First Point.

'Behold an angel of the Lord appeared in sleep to Joseph' (St. Matt. ii.).

Let us think of the purity and holiness of St. Joseph. He was often in the company of angels. No less than four times in his life we are told angels were bending over him as he lay asleep. They may have come much oftener. Let us desire to have angels guarding us in sleep, so that in the words of the Church we may obtain this grace from God:

'Keep us like shrines beneath Thine eye,
Pure in our foes' despite.'°

The devil likes to tempt people at night, because he is the prince of darkness; but though he can tempt, he can never overcome those who call on their angels to help them.

° Compline.

Second Point.

'Saying, Arise, and take the Child and His Mother, and fly into Egypt' (St. Matt. ii.).

What an extraordinary command this must have seemed to St. Joseph! He was to take a most dangerous journey into a foreign country; and that not alone, but having under his charge a young Mother and a little Child.

What a lesson we learn here of obedience! How often do we make difficulties on the plea that the command given is unwise or unreasonable! But it was God Himself who was speaking to St. Joseph, and we see the order He gave: 'Arise' at once, in the middle of the night, without any preparation; no time to take leave of friends or find any help. Am I ready to do God's will at once?

Third Point.

'For it will come to pass that Herod will seek the Child to destroy Him' (St. Matt. ii.).

But might not St. Joseph have said, 'Lord, canst Thou not defend Thine own?' 'Is Thy hand shortened, that it cannot save?' (Isaias lix.)

'And fly into Egypt.'

'But was it not out of Egypt Thou didst bring Thy chosen people? Canst Thou not again, as Thou didst then, "put down Thy adversaries in the multitude of Thy glory; send forth Thy wrath, and devour them like stubble"?' (Exodus xv.)

But we are very sure St. Joseph never argued with God, but obeyed simply, promptly, entirely. Let me ask Him to help me to follow His blessed example.

Colloquy.—Resolution.

FEBRUARY 4.

THE FLIGHT INTO EGYPT.

First Prelude.—Imagine you see the desert through which the Holy Family had to pass.

Second Prelude.—
> 'Be done sweet will of Thine,
>   Jesu Divine;
> Love of my heart,
>   Make Thy will mine.'

First Point.

'Who arose, and took the Child and His Mother by night' (St. Matt. ii.).

Let us contemplate this wonderful picture—home, friends, and country forsaken in a moment, and the most favoured beings on this earth—those over whom angels watched, those who were infinitely greater than all the princes of the earth—flying as fugitives before the puny power of King Herod, a vassal of imperial Rome. Were there no angels, nor 'a flaming sword turning every way, to keep the way of the tree of life'? (Gen. iii.)

Let us adore Him who says to us, 'My thoughts are not your thoughts, nor your ways My ways' (Isaias lv.).

Second Point.

'And took the Child and His Mother.'

There was no question of *their* obedience. The angel did not come to Mary; he came to the head of the family, knowing that the Mother and the Child would obey him without a question. And then our dear Lady underwent her Second Dolour. Clasping her Child to her breast, she swiftly prepared to fly. His life was threatened; what anguish came into her soul! Was the hour of sacrifice already come? Could she and St. Joseph indeed save Him from His enemies?

Do I try to save Him from His enemies? Do I always take His part? Am I ever 'ashamed of Him before men,' by not defending the faith or by doing wrong from fear of scorn or ridicule?

Third Point.
'The Child and His Mother.'
There is a beautiful tradition that the Holy Family took refuge one night in a robber's cave. They were too poor to be

robbed. A child of the same age as our Lord, and called Dimas, was suffering from leprosy, that terrible and incurable disease. Our Lady advised his mother to wash him in the same water in which she had washed *her* Child, and, lo, the leprosy disappeared.

Do I take care to bathe my soul, not in water, but in the Precious Blood, that 'cleanseth from all sin'? (St. John i.) Do I try to gain the grace attached to frequent confession—great purity of heart?

Colloquy.—Resolution.

FEBRUARY 5.

THE HOLY FAMILY IN EGYPT.

First Prelude.—Imagine you see the broad river Nile, and the palm-trees of Egypt.

Second Prelude.—Jesus, Sun of Justice, have mercy on me.

First Point.

'And retired into Egypt' (St. Matt. ii.).

The Holy Family remained some years in exile. It is supposed they dwelt at Heliopolis, or the City of the Sun, where stood the Temple of the Sun. In it the Egyptians paid worship. Now, indeed, the city deserved its name; for the Sun of Justice was within it—'He that sendeth forth light, and it goeth, and it obeyeth Him with trembling' (Baruch iii.).

The Egyptians also worshipped idols of wood and stone; and tradition says, when the Divine Child passed by these temples, the idols fell to the ground.

God had said by His prophet, 'The Lord will enter into Egypt, and the idols of Egypt shall be moved at His presence' (Isaias xix.).

Second Point.

'That it might be fulfilled which the Lord spoke by the prophet, saying, Out of Egypt have I called My Son' (St. Matt. ii.).

We can well imagine how our Lady and St. Joseph must have thought and talked together of the wonderful events that had passed in Egypt in the olden time. Perhaps they rested on the banks of the Nile when the day's labour was over; and the little Jesus sat on His Mother's lap, and listened to the wondrous tale, 'more delicate and lovely a thousand times in His human loveliness than the fairest snowy lotus-flower that was ever cradled on the bosom of the Nile.'*

Seventeen centuries before, 'famine prevailed in the whole world; but there was bread in all the land of Egypt' (Genesis xli.). And in Egypt now was the Living Bread.

And then Mary remembered the ancient words: 'And when there also they began to be famished, the people cried to Pharao for food. And he said to them, Go to Joseph, and do all that he shall say to you' (Genesis xli.).

And now another Joseph, her own beloved spouse, was the guardian of that Bread of

* Father Faber.

which 'he that eateth shall live for ever' (St. John vi.).

Third Point.

'And when Herod was dead, behold an angel of the Lord appeared in sleep to Joseph in Egypt, saying, Arise, and take the Child and His Mother, and go into the land of Israel; for they are dead that sought the life of the Child' (St. Matt. ii.).

And so there was a second Exodus or *going out* from Egypt; this time not a great armed multitude, but three poor obscure people.

And they crossed the Red Sea, type of the Precious Blood, and went into the desert; and Mary and Joseph did not need the 'pillar of a cloud by day, and a pillar of fire by night to show the way,' for the Lord Himself, holding their hands or resting in their arms, was the 'guide of their journey' (Exodus xiii.).

And perchance on the shore of that Red Sea, when they had safely passed, Mary, re-

FEBRUARY FIFTH.

membering the Song of Miriam, sang again *her* Magnificat, and they passed the spot where first fell the manna from heaven (Exodus xvi.), the type of the true Bread that now was with them. And they went by the place where Moses struck the rock, and the water gushed out; and now He was with them who saith, ' If any man thirst, let him come unto Me and drink' (St. John vii.).

And as they journeyed on they came to the spot where once the ' sign was set up : whoever being struck shall look on it shall live' (Numbers xxi.) ; and He was there who soon should say Himself, ' As Moses lifted up the serpent in the desert, so must the Son of Man be lifted up, that whosoever believeth in him shall not perish' (St. John iii.).

How our hearts ought to swell with love and gratitude towards our dear Lord ! What deep-rooted confidence we should have in Jesus !

Colloquy.—Resolution.

February 6.

RETURN OF THE HOLY FAMILY.

First Prelude.—Imagine you see the sandy desert along which they have to pass.

Second Prelude.—Show me Thy ways, O Lord, and teach me Thy paths.

First Point.

'Who arose, and took the Child and His Mother, and came into the land of Israel' (St. Matt. ii.).

Many beautiful traditions are told of the journey of the Holy Family through the desert; and this mystery has been 'a fountain of poetry and art to the Church at large.'*

It is said that leatless trees were clothed with rich foliage, and bent their branches to shelter the blessed pilgrims; that grass sprang up at our Lady's feet, and when St. Joseph, seeing his dear ones suffer, prayed to God, a well of water gushed forth beside him.

* Father Faber.

Let us contemplate this lovely picture:
'There is the sunset in the wilderness, its
light reflected on Joseph's eyes; and then
there is Jesus sleeping on His Mother's lap;
and the round moon above, and the glittering well, and the whispering palm, and night
breathing heavily over the yellow sands.'*

Second Point.

'But hearing that Archelaus reigned in
Judea in the room of Herod his father, he
was afraid to go thither, and being warned in
sleep retired into the quarters of Galilee' (St.
Matt. ii.).

Still our Lord would not exert His divine
power against His persecutors. He would
suffer what His elect were afterwards to suffer, the oppression of the wicked.

Shall we, then, be dismayed if we see the
Church or the Saints or the Vicar of Christ
persecuted? Shall we be cast down if our
faith be mocked at and ridiculed, or if we

* Father Faber.

find certain ways of worldly advancement blocked before us because of our religion? No doubt the world of that day would have made merry over St. Joseph and the little Child hiding themselves for fear of Archelaus.

The Church, like her Head, can afford to be patient:

> 'Bide thou thy time,
> Watch with meek eyes the race of pride and crime;
> Sit in the gate, and be the heathen's jest,
> Smiling and self-possest.
> O thou to whom is pledged a victor's sway,
> Bide thou the victor's day.'°

Am I trying to do as our Lord bids me? Am I patient, and do I rejoice, if 'accounted worthy to suffer reproach for the name of Jesus'? (Acts v.)

Third Point.

'And coming, he dwelt in a city called Nazareth, that it might be fulfilled which was said by the prophets, That He shall be called a Nazarite' (St. Matt. ii.).

° Cardinal Newman.

And so, after their perilous journey and years of exile, the Holy Family reached their home, the spot that was ever dear to Mary, because there the Word was made flesh.

Every time we return home after a journey we should think of that everlasting rest, towards which we are all travelling, and we should pray, and try to be ready for it:

'And heaven, the heart's true home, will come at last.'°

Colloquy.—Resolution.

February 7.

THE HOLY CHILDHOOD.

First Prelude.—Imagine you see the holy house in which Jesus and His parents dwelt.

Second Prelude.—

'Teach, O teach me, Holy Child,
Teach me to resemble Thee.'

First Point.

'And the Child grew' (St. Luke ii.).

° Father Faber.

He grew like other children; He learned to walk, to run about; He was the joy of His Mother's heart, the consolation of His foster-father.

Am I the source of joy to those who have the charge of me? Can they look hopefully to my future because I grow in grace?

Second Point.

'And waxed strong, full of wisdom' (St. Luke ii.).

There are many beautiful legends concerning the childhood of our dear Lord.

They say that He sometimes played with the other children; and they looked up to Him, and when any dispute arose among them they would say, 'Let us go to the sweet-tempered one;* let us ask Jesus, the Son of Mary, and let Him decide;' and He always made peace.

Do I try always to make peace? Do I carefully avoid that detestable habit of repeating

* Eamus ad suavitatem.

to one person what another has said of him or her, which is sure to lead to mischief?

Third Point.

'And the grace of God was in Him' (St. Luke ii.).

When we read these words do we not say, 'Happy Mother and foster-father! happy relatives and friends, who dwelt near Him and saw Him in His lovely childhood!' But we can share their joy if we become familiar with Him, and dwell in His company. And we will strive to imitate Him, for then we shall know Him; and of those who admired Him in Nazareth, none knew Him but His parents. O, then, let us 'follow on, that we may know the Lord' (Osee vi.).

Colloquy.—Resolution.

FEBRUARY 8.

GOING UP TO JERUSALEM.

First Prelude.—Imagine you see the road along which the Holy Family are travelling.

Second Prelude.—Make me to walk, O Lord, in the way of Thy law.

First Point.

'And His parents went every year to Jerusalem at the solemn day of the Pasch' (St. Luke ii.).

We see how faithfully Joseph and Mary obeyed the law, although they knew that with the coming of the Divine Child ' old things were passed away' (2 Cor. v.).

Are we careful in obeying rules or customs, or are we apt to say, 'There is no use in doing that? It ought to be changed and done away with; therefore it can be neglected.'

Second Point.

'And when He was twelve years old' (St. Luke ii.).

The Jewish law ordained that all who were over twelve years old must come to visit the Temple at the time of the Pasch. Women were not obliged to go at all; but we can easily imagine that our Lady would never, of her own will, separate herself for an hour from her Child. The long painful journey was nothing to her in comparison.

Is it a pain to me when I cannot enjoy the presence of Jesus in His Sacrament? Do I neglect to visit Him?

Third Point.

'They going up into Jerusalem according to the custom of the feast' (St. Luke ii.).

Again we contemplate the Holy Family entering the Temple, and this time the beautiful Child walks by His Mother's side. How full must have been the hearts of our Lady and St. Joseph whenever they went into the Temple with Jesus! How all the words of the old prophecies must have rushed back to their minds, and how they must have inwardly exclaimed, in the words of King Solomon, 'Is it, then, to be thought that God should indeed dwell upon earth? for heaven, and the heaven of heavens, cannot contain thee; how much less this house!' (3 Kings viii.)

Our churches are as holy as the Temple was at this moment; for they possess no less truly the presence of Jesus.

Am I very reverent in them? Many, on entering a church, say, 'How terrible is this place! This is no other but the house of God and the gate of heaven' (Gen. xxviii.). While my knee touches the ground, does my heart honour Him?

Colloquy.—Resolution.

February 9.
THE LOSS OF THE CHILD JESUS.

First Prelude. — Imagine you see the crowd of pilgrims on the road to Nazareth.

Second Prelude.—
> 'Stay with us, Saviour so holy;
> Stay with us now evermore.'

First Point.

'And having fulfilled the days, when they

returned, the Child Jesus remained in Jerusalem, and His parents knew it not' (St. Luke ii.).

The Paschal week had ended, and crowds of pilgrims were quitting the holy city. In order to prevent confusion each tribe was told off to depart by itself, the men by one gate, the women by another, but children might go with either. Thus our Lady thought the Child was with St. Joseph, and he thought Jesus was with His Mother. Only when they halted for the night was the loss discovered, and our Lady's Third Dolour met her.

We cannot understand her grief, because we cannot comprehend her love. 'To what shall I equal thee, that I may comfort thee, O virgin daughter of Sion?' (Lam. ii.)

Second Point.

'And thinking He was in the company, they came a day's journey' (St. Luke ii.).

We can at least catch a glimpse of our Lady's trouble. Even the very young meet at times with disappointment, and are called upon to part with those they love; and all can pity a mother who has lost her child. Any such grief is terrible. But there was never a child like unto Jesus, and never a mother like Mary.

Imagine the agony, the suspense! What had become of Him? Had His enemies seized on Him? Was He suffering, and away from her? She who for twelve long years had smoothed His hair and kissed His lips ere He lay down to sleep. Was He really gone?

Have I not lost my Jesus by sin, and has it been to me a pain beyond all other pains?

Third Point.

'And sought Him among their kinsfolk and acquaintance' (St. Luke ii.).

There is a peculiar bitterness in repeated disappointment, for 'Hope deferred maketh the heart sick' (Prov. xiii.). But patience and cheerfulness *then* are golden.

She went from place to place, and the answer was, 'No, we have not seen Him.' Then, no doubt, there would be useless questions and wonderment, perhaps blame of the Child; and all these were sending the sword deeper into Mary's soul.

Do I do my best to comfort the sorrowful? Do I try to enter into the troubles of others, and not to be occupied entirely with self? Am I sweet-tempered under disappointment?

Colloquy.—Resolution.

FEBRUARY 10.

OUR LADY AND ST. JOSEPH SEEK THE CHILD.

First Prelude.—Imagine you see the streets of Jerusalem.

Second Prelude.—'And after this exile show to us the fruit of thy womb, Jesus.'

First Point.

'And not finding Him' (St. Luke ii.).

The sorrowful Mother and her spouse now

begin to retrace their steps. They cannot wait till the morning. They do not fear the dangers of the road, for the worst that can happen to them has taken place. They have lost their all, and deep grief, like deep love, knows no fear. St. Joseph's heart is almost broken in witnessing the grief of our Lady, and it is a fresh sorrow to her to see the sorrow of Joseph. They think of another midnight journey flying into Egypt; but that was nothing in comparison, for Jesus was with them: now they are alone.

Second Point.

'They returned into Jerusalem' (St. Luke ii.).

Imagine these broken-hearted parents re-entering Jerusalem.

Might not our Lady have said, in the words that Noemi used of old, 'I went out full, and the Lord hath brought me back empty; the Almighty hath quite filled me with bitterness'? (Ruth i.)

They did not tarry to rest or to take food. They went, we cannot doubt, first to the Temple to pray. He was not there. Their footsteps only woke the echoes in the great courts where but yesterday He had been by their side. Then they went swiftly, yet always calmly, about the city, seeking, but never finding, as day shadowed into night and night melted into day. And ever in Mary's ears the words were ringing, 'Thine own soul a sword shall pierce.' How dearly we should love our Lady, for all her sorrows were caused by our sins!

Third Point.

We have thought of the sorrow of Mary and Joseph, but let us now think of the sorrow of Jesus. The Saints tell us it was one of the chief sufferings of His life, for His love for His Mother was even greater than her love for Him. The parting from her was terrible; and besides, He had to give the pain, she but to bear it.

Where was our Lord during those three days? The Saints believe He begged His bread, that He might know the depth of poverty, and out of the alms given to Him He gave to the poor. He slept on the bare ground. The Creator of all things was a beggar in His own world. He was thus beginning to be 'despised of men;' and shall I be proud, shall I refuse a little humiliation?

Colloquy.—Resolution.

February 11.

THE FINDING IN THE TEMPLE.

First Prelude.—Imagine you see the Temple of Jerusalem.

Second Prelude.—O my Lord and my God, draw my heart away from all other things that are not of Thee.

First Point.

'And it came to pass that after three days they found Him' (St. Luke ii.).

What joy must have filled the immaculate heart of Mary and the holy soul of Joseph! The loss had lasted so long that it is possible our Lady and St. Joseph thought it might be God's will to remove their treasure altogether from their keeping; and suddenly they found Him.

All sorrow sent by God and patiently borne is sure to end in joy, if not on earth, in heaven. 'They that sow in tears shall reap in joy' (Ps. cxxvi.).

Second Point.

'In the Temple, sitting in the midst of the doctors, hearing them and asking them questions' (St. Luke ii.).

We may be certain that during the three days both Mary and Joseph went often to the Temple to pray for strength in their sorrow. And on the fourth day they were inspired to enter by the eastern gate. Close to this was the Academy, a spacious room in which the doctors or teachers of the law sat to hear and answer questions; and as they pass by this room, the 'Mother's ear has caught a sound—it is the voice of Jesus.'*

Third Point.

Do I want to find Jesus? There is a sure way to do so—prayer and the Sacraments. 'If thou seek Him, thou shalt find Him' (1 Paral. xxviii.).

'And all that heard Him were astonished at His wisdom and answers' (St. Luke ii.).

The Divine Child was conversing with His creatures as if He were their inferior. A Child before aged and learned men—modest, gentle, humble.

What a model for the young before their superiors and before the aged! What a contrast to a rude, forward, offhand manner! What were our Lord's questions to the doc-

° Father Faber.

tors? The Saints believe He questioned them about the Messias; and when He found that they expected a king and a warrior, who should restore the temporal glory of the Jews, He quoted the words of the prophecies, and thus compelled them to see that it was not according to their ideas God would fulfil His promise.

If I ever have to teach the faith to others, or to show others that they are wrong, let me be sure to do so with prudence and meekness.

Colloquy.—Resolution.

FEBRUARY 12.

GOING DOWN TO NAZARETH.

First Prelude.—Imagine you see the gate of Jerusalem, through which the Holy Family pass.

Second Prelude.—Holy Child, make me to follow Thy example.

First Point.

'And seeing Him, they wondered. And His Mother said to Him, Son, why hast Thou done so to us? Behold Thy father and I have sought Thee sorrowing' (St. Luke ii.).

Our Lady could not have suffered as she did in her Third Dolour if she had understood the meaning of our Lord's disappearance.

A very holy religious, who meditated much on this mystery, believed that the angels were not allowed to enlighten her.*

So she spoke to Him who for twelve years had been her submissive loving Child, but whom she also knew was her God; and she sought to know His will, that she might do it.

Do we try to find out the will of God in all simplicity only, that we may do it? or do we try and twist it so as to suit our own way?

Second Point.

'And He said to them, How is it that ye

* Sister Mary of Agreda.

sought Me? Did you not know that I must be about My Father's business?' (St. Luke ii.)

Our Lord spoke these words to teach us that He is to be first with all His creatures; that there are times in our lives when we may have to make the choice between Him and those nearest and dearest to us. This was often the case, even with children, in the first ages of the Church, when they were converted to the faith. It is so in our own day in heathen countries like China; and in many other instances even the young are called on to be about 'their Father's business.'

Third Point.

'And they understood not the word that He spoke to them; and He went down with them, and came to Nazareth' (St. Luke ii.).

Our Lord, by remaining in Jerusalem for three days, had taught us that there is one exception to the law of obedience to parents, and one only, and that save when God's will clearly calls us away, we should always dwell in the shelter of our homes and render obedience; and this even if it cost us much, and if we think we could do great good by acting otherwise. It would seem as if our Lord desired to begin 'His Father's business' at the age of twelve; but when He saw His parents did not understand, He went with them to Nazareth. And He did this to teach us how pleasant submission is in the eyes of God.

Do I believe that submission is so great a virtue? Do my acts show that I believe it?

Colloquy.—Resolution.

February 13.

THE HOLY HOUSE AT NAZARETH.

First Prelude.—Imagine you see the holy house at Nazareth.

Second Prelude.—Jesus, meek and humble of Heart, make my heart like unto Thine.

First Point.

'And came to Nazareth' (St. Luke ii.).

We are not left to conjecture what the holy house was like. It yet remains on the earth, having been miraculously transported to Loretto in Italy, now about a day's journey from Rome. Pilgrims daily visit it, and for ages Saints have gone there to pour out their hearts' devotion and love. It would be hard to find a human habitation as poor as that in which dwelt Jesus and His parents: stones put together with rude cement, an earthen floor, holes in the walls for windows, and the whole dwelling small and narrow. And here the God of heaven and earth passed eighteen years after His finding in the Temple, and at least several years before that. And we seek after riches and comforts, or at least we complain of hardships, of privations!

Shall I not try to gain that blessing of my Lord, 'Blessed are ye poor'? (St. Luke vi.)

Second Point.

'And was subject to them' (St. Luke ii.).

We have marvelled to see Him obedient as an infant and a little child, but now we see Him obedient as a boy, a youth, and even to manhood. It was a perfect and real obedience. He said of Himself, 'Behold I come to do Thy will, O God.' And He saw in Mary and Joseph's will that of God. Thus we can never err as long as we obey lawful superiors, because they stand to us in the place of God.

Let us, then, earnestly strive after obedience. ' O my Saviour, who wast subject to Thy parents for thirty years, who wouldst be born, live, and die in obedience, make me follow Thy example, and spend my life in continual obedience.'

Third Point.

'And Jesus advanced in wisdom and age and grace with God and men' (St. Luke ii.).

Here is the perfect example our Lord has

left to all those who are receiving education. He could not actually advance, for He was all-perfect for ever; but He let His wisdom gradually manifest itself. The older we grow the better we should be, the nearer we should be to God, and the more consolation we should give to those who govern us.

Can those who have charge of me say, as St. Paul did of his spiritual children, 'You are our glory and joy'? (1 Thes. ii.)

Colloquy.—Resolution.

February 14.

THE HIDDEN LIFE.

First Prelude.—Imagine you see the town of Nazareth.

Second Prelude.—
> 'Heart of the Holy Child,
> Hide me in Thee.'

First Point.

'Is not this the carpenter's son'? (St. Luke xiii.)

Let us contemplate our dear Lord in the workshop of St. Joseph. He was learning a trade, learning to support Himself. He had to earn His own bread. He came to share our life, and so the Sinless accepted the penalty of sin: 'In the sweat of thy face shalt thou eat bread' (Genesis iii.).

St. Joseph gave Him orders, taught Him how to use the saw, the plane, and the hammer. No doubt He went with His father or alone to take back the work to the rich and receive wages, and was often kept waiting and found fault with.

Do I love the poor? Do I treat them with reverence? for they are the very images of my Lord and Saviour.

He loved them so that He chose always to be one of them, and never to be rich. Love of the poor is a mark of sanctity, and for those we love we make sacrifices willingly.

Second Point.

'I am poor and in labour, from my youth' (Ps. lxxxvii. 16).

Let us well study this mystery. Jesus came to teach men and to save the world. His life was to last only thirty-three years, and thirty of these may be summed up in these words. He was poor, laborious, unknown, and obedient, and He left us an example that we should follow His steps. Let us, therefore, love poverty, and rejoice if we are poor.

We should be industrious, and we should hold those who labour at what is called menial work in honour, and be glad to share in it if it be God's will for us; and if we love poverty we shall love to be unknown, for the world always despises the poor. We must also, and above all things, be 'poor in spirit;' and this the truly obedient always are.

Third Point.

'Is not His Mother called Mary?' (St. Matt. xiii.)

We feel sure that our Lord aided His Mother in the household cares—swept the floor, prepared the fire, washed the cups and platters. Those same cups from which His divine lips drank are at Loretto still.

Tradition says He went with His Mother to the fountain, both to draw water and carry it home in the large earthen pitchers used for this purpose in the East, or to wash their linen.

Water was scarce at Nazareth, and the well distant from the town. Nazareth has changed little since our Lady's time, and pious pilgrims, beholding the Eastern women and children in their dress of white or bright blue or red cotton climbing the steep hill on which the house of Mary stood, have realised strongly the wondrous humility of Jesus and Mary.

Let me, therefore, say from my heart, 'From the fear of being despised deliver me, Jesus.'

Colloquy.—Resolution.

February 15.

Ash-Wednesday—The Meaning of this Day.

First Prelude. — Imagine you see the desolate place, covered with thorns and thistles, into which Adam and Eve were driven.

Second Prelude.—Have mercy on me, O God, after Thy great goodness.

First Point.

'Remember, O man, that thou art dust.'

This day takes its name from the custom of the Church of blessing ashes and placing them on the heads of the faithful, the priest repeating to each person the words said by God to Adam after his fall, 'Dust thou art, and unto dust shalt thou return' (Gen. iii.); and the Church bids each of us to 'remember' this. It is the yearly warning that our Holy Mother the Church gives to us that we must die.

Do I remember this truth that I must die, and I know not when or how? Death comes to all: the baby, the little child, the schoolboy or girl, the young man and the maiden, are often called away. Death does not always wait for old age or long sickness. It comes early, it comes swiftly, and no one is truly wise who is not ready for the call, come when it may.

Second Point.

'Dust thou art, and unto dust shalt thou return' (Gen. iii.).

Why did God say these words to Adam? Because pride had filled his heart, and he who had been 'taken out of the earth' aspired in his folly to be equal to the uncreated God, who was and who is and who is to come. Therefore God humbled Adam, and reminded him that he was the work of His hands, formed from the dust.

Let us, then, have a horror of pride, of exalting ourselves, thinking much of even our best deeds. 'Why is earth and ashes proud?' (Eccles. x.)

'Every proud man is an abomination to the Lord' (Prov. xvi.); and the Church, to teach us humility, lays ashes on our heads. The best way to prepare for death is to be humble, for the kingdom of heaven belongs to the poor in spirit; let us each, therefore, say to ourselves, in the words of the *Imitation of Christ,* 'Learn, O dust, to obey; earth and clay that thou art, learn to humble thyself.'

Third Point.

'He remembereth that we are but dust' (Ps. cii.).

Do we not, indeed, know and feel that we are but dust?

What mean, vile, and base things are these hearts of ours, so hard to others, so ungrateful towards our God! Sometimes we realise this, and a sense of our own misery throws us into despondency; then let us take comfort, remembering that our merciful God knoweth whereof we are made.

'He remembereth that we are but dust.'

He bears with us, waits for us, if we may so say makes excuses for us; and the day will come for each, if only we are faithful to God's grace, when we shall no longer be dust, when 'we shall be changed, and this corruptible must put on incorruption' (1 Cor. xv.).

Colloquy.—Resolution.

February 16.

FIRST THURSDAY IN LENT—THE RIGHT USE OF LENT.

First Prelude.—As yesterday.

Second Prelude.—By Thy Passion and Thy Cross, O Lord, bring me to the glory of Thy Resurrection.

First Point.

'Sanctify a fast, call a solemn assembly, gather together the people, sanctify the Church, gather together the little ones' (Joel ii.).

These words of the prophet are adopted by the Church in her Mass for Ash-Wednesday. We see, therefore, even the young are intended by her to keep this holy season.

'It is good for a man when he hath borne the yoke from his youth,' says the prophet (Lam. iii.); and none lead such happy lives as those who early drink in the spirit of the Church, and make her ways their ways. Let us, then, enter into the spirit of our Holy Mother, and spend more time in prayer during Lent, and increase our acts of mortification; and if in earnest we

> 'Wait along the penance-tide
>   Of solemn fast and prayer;
> . . . . hide
> In our own hearts, and count the wounds
>   Of passion and of pride,'°

we shall certainly cry to our God for help, and desire, as far as lies in our power, to do penance.

° Cardinal Newman.

Second Point.

'When you fast, be not as the hypocrites, sad' (St. Matt. vi.).

There is nothing sad in God's service. The more we serve Him, and the longer, the more convinced we are of this truth. The young often think religion is very dull and hard, and that continual watchfulness over self is wearisome. Yet the most austere Saints are always the most joyful, for joy and happiness do not consist in outward things; they have their well-spring in the heart, and the nearer we are to God the more joyful we shall be. 'The meek shall increase their joy in the Lord' (Isaias xxix.).

Third Point.

'And as in Adam all die, so also in Christ all shall be made alive' (1 Cor. xv.).

The fast of Lent is instituted to enable us to prepare worthily to keep the greatest of all our feasts, the anniversary of our Lord's

Resurrection; and by preparing ourselves well for death, we shall also prepare for our glorious resurrection. Perhaps some of us, shrinking back from the thought of penance, may say, in the words of one of our poets:

> 'I have walked this world these two months past
>   With quick free step, loud voice, and youth's light cheer;
> And dull and weary were the shadows cast
>   From the dark Cross and Lent's dim portals near.'

But if we persevere as he did, we also ere long may say with him:

> 'O joy of all our joys, to be bereft
>   Of our false power to make the world so dear!
> O joy of all our joys, to be thus left
>   In our wild years with none but Jesus near!'*

Can I not, then, make a brave resolution to gain some special graces during Lent, and, offering my determination to God, ask Him for help to keep it?

Colloquy.—Resolution.

* Father Faber.

February 17.

FIRST FRIDAY IN LENT—OUR LORD IN THE DESERT.

First Prelude.—Imagine you see the desert in which our Lord passed forty days and nights.

Second Prelude.—Heart of Jesus, filled with bitterness for our sakes, have mercy on me.

First Point.

'And He was in the desert' (St. Mark i.).

Let us try and bring before our minds what a desert is. It is an enormous tract of sand, uncultivated and uninhabited, without trees or herbage, except in spots far apart from each other, where there may be a well, round which a little grass may spring up. Great rocks sometimes rise in these deserts, under which the traveller can find a slight shelter from the burning sun. It is easy to lose the way in a desert, and travellers who have passed through deserts even in parties speak of the way in which the awful solitude of the scene oppressed them. And our dear Lord was alone in the desert for love of me.

Can I bear to be alone for love of Him? to spend a little time alone with Him in prayer? to be left alone rather than share some forbidden pleasure? to keep silence in honour of His long silence in the desert?

Second Point.

'And He was with beasts' (St. Mark i.).

The desert is the abode of wild beasts and birds of prey. 'Wild beasts shall rest there; it shall be the habitation of dragons; thither are the kites gathered together' (Isaias xiii. 84).

This was the company that now surrounded our Lord. No longer the peaceful ox and ass that witnessed His birth, or the little doves that went with Him to the Temple, or the sheep and the lambs, the meek lamb, emblem of Himself; but He was with the 'evil beasts,' as they are called in Holy Scripture.

Was our Lord afraid of them? His own hand had made them—'the beasts of the earth according to their kind' (Gen. i.). We cannot doubt that they owned their Creator, and gave Him their dumb homage. The passions of our poor fallen nature are often like wild beasts, such as anger, revenge, and others.

Do I resolutely subdue them before my Lord? When He comes into my heart, does He ever find it like a desert, and full of thoughts and feelings in rebellion against Him? What should I do, then?

Third Point.

'And He ate nothing in those days, and He was hungry' (St. Luke iv.).

Very often the poor have to suffer hunger, but they have never had to suffer like our Lord did; for by His omnipotence He sustained His life, and yet ever felt the pangs of hunger.

And can I not deny myself some little comfort, practise some slight mortification, during the short time of Lent, for love of Him who for love of me 'fasted forty days and forty nights'? And perhaps that self-denial or mortification may enable me to give some little alms to the poor, whose frequent hunger makes them more than ever the images of Jesus, who, 'being very rich, became poor for your sakes' (1 Cor. viii.). He asks us to pity Him in the persons of His poor.

> 'Hungry, by whom Saints are fed
> With the eternal Living Bread;
> Thirsty, from whose pierced side
> Healing waters spring and glide;
> Cold and bare He comes who never
> May put off His robe of light;
> Homeless, who must dwell for ever
> Within the Father's bosom bright.'°

Colloquy.—Resolution.

February 18.

FIRST SATURDAY IN LENT—OUR LORD TEMPTED BY THE DEVIL.

First Prelude.—As yesterday.

° Keble.

Second Prelude.—Jesus, tempted in the desert, have mercy on me.

'And was tempted by Satan' (St. Mark i.).

We often complain of temptations, and sometimes we say they are too hard for us, and we cannot resist them. But we can, because our Lord has taught us the way. For our sakes He was tempted. He could not sin; the devil never could have prevailed over Him; but for our sakes He went through all the pain, all the humiliation. For our sakes He suffered the Evil One—ten thousand times more abhorrent to Him than the tiger or the vulture—to approach Him.

Shall I not take fresh courage, and 'give not place to the devil'? (Ephes. iv.)

Second Point.

'And the tempter coming, said to Him, If Thou be the Son of God, command that these stones be made bread' (St. Matt. iv.).

Our Lord was faint with hunger. He was suffering more than any human being has ever endured from this pain. Pressed by hunger, Esau sold his birthright. Great hunger has made mothers forget their children, men their humanity, and Christians their God. Yet to end this suffering our Lord would not work a miracle. He who has worked that perpetual miracle, whereby bread becomes His Divine Flesh, would not spare Himself one pang of the hunger He was enduring, that we afterwards might feed on the 'Bread of the strong.' And also He was expiating our sins, the many sins that come from an over-indulgence in food.

How earnestly I should resolve never to commit any sin of this kind!

Third Point.

'And Jesus answered him, It is written that man liveth not by bread alone, but by every word of God' (St. Luke iv.).

Our Lord teaches us to despise earthly comforts when they interfere with the service of God.

Sometimes Catholics find it hard to keep the laws of the Church about fasting and abstinence.

Human respect and discomfort are in their way; then the thought of the long fast of their sinless Master will strengthen them, and gladly they will 'confess Him before men,' or by brave self-denial 'fast to their Father who is in secret.'

Colloquy.—Resolution.

February 19.

FIRST SUNDAY IN LENT—THE SAME (CONTINUED).

First Prelude.—As before.

Second Prelude.—From the desire of being esteemed deliver me, Jesus.

First Point.

'And the devil led Him into a high mountain, and showed Him all the kingdoms of the world in a moment of time. And he said to Him, To Thee will I give all this power, and the glory of them; for to me they are delivered, and to whom I will I give them. If Thou, therefore, wilt adore before me, all shall be Thine' (St. Luke iv.).

The young often think their elders exaggerate the dangers of the world.

To them it looks, as the apple looked to Eve, 'fair to the eyes and delightful to behold,' and they do not see its hidden dangers. Let us listen, then, to the archenemy saying, 'All the power and glory are delivered to me.' Satan is the 'prince of this world;' and therefore we must hate the world and despise it, bear its ridicule and its scorn rather than give up a duty, or consent to a guilty pleasure. For the world does not consist only of a round of gaieties; love of the world means the love of external things, apart from the love of God, and in opposition to His holy will.

Second Point.

'And Jesus answering said to him, It is written, Thou shalt adore the Lord thy God, and Him only shalt thou serve.'

How calm and majestic was the answer of our Lord! Even the feeblest among us can imitate it, for in His strength, armed with His grace, each of us can have great power over Satan. 'God is able to make all grace abound in you' (2 Cor ix.).

Third Point.

'And he brought Him to Jerusalem, and set Him on a pinnacle of the Temple; and he said to Him, If Thou be the Son of God, cast Thyself from hence; for it is written that He hath given His angels charge over Thee, that they keep Thee. And that in their hands they shall bear Thee up, lest perhaps Thou dash Thy foot against a stone' (St. Luke iv.).

The devil has two ways of ensnaring us: first, by temptations to do evil; and secondly, by inducing us to do things in themselves good in the wrong way, or time, or place. St. Paul says, 'Satan himself transformeth himself into an angel of light' (2 Cor. xi.).

Finding that our Lord met the two first temptations by the words of Scripture, Satan then tried to twist other sacred words to his own purpose. How often does he tempt us in like manner! He wants us to pray when we should be at work or study, and then distracts us when the time of prayer has come; or he leads us to despise the common duties of our life, by firing our ambition to do some great thing to which God has not called us.

'O most sweet Jesus, the refuge and strength of all who are tempted, be careful of me, O Lord, that I may not fear what malignant spirits can do to me, but that I may set Thee always in my sight; for Thou art on my right hand, that I may not be moved.*

Colloquy.—Resolution.

* *Paradisus Animæ.*

February 20.

First Monday after the First Sunday in Lent—The Angels in the Desert.

First Prelude.—Imagine you see a number of angels approaching our Lord in the desert.

Second Prelude.—May what I ask be done as Thou wilt, when Thou wilt, and how Thou wilt!

First Point.

'And Jesus answering said to him, It is said, Thou shalt not tempt the Lord thy God' (St. Luke iv.).

And thus does our Lord teach us how to overcome all those delusions and snares of the devil of which we thought yesterday.

All that we do and desire to do must be conformed to the adorable will of God, and we know that His will shall be always made known to us by our lawful superiors.

Second Point.

'Then the devil left Him' (St. Matt. iv.).

The arch-enemy was conquered, and had to flee away.

And so can it always be with us. The devil cannot conquer us unless we choose. His 'head has been crushed' by our Lady and her Son, and we can trample the serpent under our feet. One of our living poets* shows us in the most powerful manner the impotence of the devils when they are boldly resisted; and he adds:

> 'When some child of grace, angel or saint,
> Pure and upright in his integrity
> Of nature, meets the demons in their raid,
> They scud away as cowards from the fight.'

The devil is a liar, and all liars are cowards. Let me, then, despise him and boldly resist him.

Third Point.

'And behold, angels came and ministered to Him' (St. Matt. iv.).

* *Dream of Gerontius*, by Cardinal Newman.

Happy angels, that were suffered to come to His succour, to feed Him and sustain Him in His feebleness! And so they also shall come to us in the hour of temptation. They are ever waiting for our call.

Sometimes when we are strongly tempted, we cry out like the servant of Eliseus: 'Alas, alas, alas, my lord, what shall we do?' But let us answer ourselves as the prophet did his servant: 'Fear not, for there are more with us than with them;' and if our eyes are opened by faith, we also shall see 'chariots of fire round about us' (1 Kings vi.); and so we too 'shall overcome in all these things, because of Him that hath loved us' (Rom. viii.).

Colloquy.—Resolution.

February 21.

**TUESDAY AFTER THE FIRST SUNDAY IN LENT—
BETHANIA.**

First Prelude.—Imagine you see the house in which our Lord was received.

Second Prelude.—' From the fear of being calumniated deliver me, Jesus !'

First Point.

'Jesus therefore, six days before the Pasch, came to Bethania. And they made Him a supper there. Mary therefore took a pound of right spikenard of great price, and anointed the feet of Jesus, and wiped His feet with her hair; and breaking the alabaster box, she poured it out upon His head; and the house was filled with the odour of the ointment' (St. John xii.; St. Mark xiv.).

The time had now came for our dear Lord to undergo His Passion and to die for us. He came up to Jerusalem and tarried awhile at Bethania, a village hard by the city, where

He had friends who loved Him. We see how they welcomed Him. How many touching reflections we can draw from the beautiful devotion of the loving Magdalene!

When we bring a gift to our Lord, is it of our most precious things, or do we only

> 'Offer what we cannot keep,
> What we have ceased to love'?°

Third Point.

'Then one of His disciples, Judas Iscariot, he that was about to betray Him, said, Why was not this ointment sold for three hundred pence and given to the poor?' (St. John xii.)

Let us learn to have a great horror of fault-finding and criticising the conduct of others. When we catch ourselves doing it, let us remember that we are following the example of Judas Iscariot. Hard judgments of others is a fault that our Lord seems specially to desire to root out of us.

This was the third time St. Magdalene

° Cardinal Newman.

had been accused before Him, and for the third time He defended her: 'Let her alone; why do you molest her? She hath wrought a good work on Me' (St. Mark xiv.).

Whenever therefore I am tempted to find fault or to criticise another, let me try to hear our Lord saying to me, 'Let her alone; why do you molest her?'

'For the poor you have always with you. What she had she hath done. Amen I say to you, wheresoever this gospel shall be preached in the whole world, that also which she hath done shall be told for a memorial of her' (St. Mark xiv.).

Again and again our Lord impresses on us the lesson that the poor represent Him. We need not envy the holy Magdalene the happiness of anointing the feet of our dear Lord. St. Austin says: 'Anoint therefore the feet of Jesus by thy good life, following in the marks which those feet of the Lord have traced.' Let us follow Him, then, in His love for the poor. 'Give to the poor,' says the Saint, 'and then thou hast wiped the feet of Jesus with thy hair;' and he adds, 'The feet which the Lord hath on earth are sorely needy.' Have I a loving merciful heart towards the poor? Do I do all I can for them? And if what I can do is very little, let me remember what our Lord said of St. Magdalene: 'What she had she hath done.' He only asks what I *can* do.

Colloquy.—Resolution.

FEBRUARY 22.

WEDNESDAY AFTER THE FIRST SUNDAY IN LENT—THE PALM-BRANCHES.

First Prelude.—Imagine you see the road along which our Lord passed strewn with palm-branches.

Second Prelude.—O Jesus my King, rule me, and I shall want nothing.

First Point.

'A great multitude, when they heard that Jesus was coming to Jerusalem, took branches of palm-trees, and went forth to meet Him, and cried, Hosanna! Blessed is He that cometh in the name of the Lord, the King of Israel' (St. John xii.).

This reception of our Lord shows us that the Jews had begun to believe in Him. He was no longer hidden. He had proclaimed His Divinity and worked many miracles; and so they welcomed Him as their King.

Do I, who know well enough He is my King, submit myself to Him? Do I let Him rule my thoughts, words, and actions, laying down my will and desires at His feet?

Second Point.

'And Jesus found a young ass, and sat upon it, that it might be fulfilled which was spoken by the prophet, saying, Tell ye the daughter of Sion, Behold, thy King cometh to thee, meek and sitting upon an ass' (St. John xii.; St. Matt. xxi.).

Even when He came as a King He came in meekness. Humility and meekness adorned Him wherever He went, in every action of His life. He accepted the homage of the Jews, for He was indeed their King—the 'King of Ages,' the 'King of Kings;' but yet He would not have the trappings of earthly grandeur and state, for 'His kingdom was not of this world.'

Never, therefore, ought any sort of superiority—such as high birth, talents, important charges—diminish our humility. Rather the higher we are in position, the more humble we should be in heart. 'The greater thou art, the more humble thyself in all things' (Eccles. iii.).

Third Point.

'And many spread their garments in the way; and others cut down boughs from the trees, and strewed them in the way' (St. Mark xi.).

These very people, who were now full of enthusiastic welcome, turned against our Lord before a week had gone by. This shows us what the friendship of the world and of the wicked is worth. Sometimes the young are easily led away by false friends, who lavish on them what they call sympathy and admiration; and often it is not till much harm is done that they find out the hollowness of these friendships. Let us learn to put our trust only in Him 'with whom there is no change nor shadow of alteration' (St. James i.). And let us never disobey or disregard the counsel of those whom He has set over us.

Colloquy.—Resolution.

February 23.

THURSDAY AFTER THE FIRST SUNDAY IN LENT—THE TEARS OF OUR LORD.

First Prelude.—Imagine you see the city of Jerusalem.

Second Prelude.—

> 'Let me mingle tears with thee,
> Mourning Him who mourned for me.'

First Point.

'And when He drew near, seeing the city, He wept over it' (St. Luke xix.).

All the homage and admiration lavished on our Lord did not give Him joy, for He knew it would not last.

Jerusalem was about to reject Him, and His Sacred Heart was filled with intense sadness, not for Himself, or for the cruel Passion that was awaiting Him, but for His people; for Jerusalem, that fair city, whose glory was about to depart from her for ever; and for all those of whom Jerusalem was a type, who should not obey His will, but reject Him.

Have I had a share in causing the tears of my Lord to flow by my resistance to His voice, speaking to me in prayer or by the counsel of superiors?

Second Point.

'Saying, If thou also hadst known, and

that in this thy day, the things that are for thy peace; but now they are hidden from thy eyes' (St. Luke xix.).

How these words portray the deep grief our dear Lord was feeling! He was, indeed, mourning over His ungrateful people, who, in their blind folly, did not recognise their Messias and their Saviour. When we sin, the snares of the devil or our own evil passions blind our eyes, so that we do not, in one sense, know what we are doing, although it is wilful ignorance on our part.

Therefore it is that the Wise Man tells us the wicked who are lost shall call out in their anguish that they were fools, because they had 'not known the way of the Lord' (Wisdom v.).

Let me, then, try, in 'this my day,' now that life is given to me, to work out my salvation; let me dread the blindness of heart which passion causes.

Third Point.

'Amen, amen I say to you, that you shall

lament and weep; but the world shall rejoice' (St. John xvi.).

On the spot where our Lord is believed to have stood when He wept over Jerusalem the Christians erected a church, called 'The Church of the Tears of Jesus.'

Our dear Lord has consecrated our tears and our weeping. He knew that we have to pass through a 'valley of tears,' and He softened its bitterness by His own precious weeping. Never let us, then, be afraid to go to Him in our sorrow, for none can console us as He will: 'As one whom the mother caresseth, so will I comfort you' (Isaias lxvi.).

Sometimes we are impatient under grief, surprised, as it were, that it should come to us. Yet our Lord has foretold it. Here we must weep and lament; but the day will come, if we are but faithful, when God Himself shall 'wipe away all tears' (Apoc. xxi.).

Colloquy.—Resolution.

February 24.

**Friday after the First Sunday in Lent—
The Children's Hosanna.**

First Prelude.—Imagine you see the Temple crowded with people.

Second Prelude.—Open Thou my lips, O Lord, and my mouth shall show forth Thy praise.

First Point.

'The children crying in the Temple, and saying, Hosanna to the Son of David!' (St. Matt. xxi.).

It seems to have been only the children who had the courage to cry Hosanna within the Temple. The people were afraid of the chief priests. Then many of them were angry with our Lord; for this day, when He entered the Temple as a King, 'He cast out them that bought and sold, and overthrew the tables of the money-changers, and the chairs of them that sold doves.'

If He was displeased at this want of reverence in the Jewish Temple, how much more must He feel about irreverence in our churches, wherein His Sacramental Presence is found!

Second Point.

'Saying to them, It is written, My house is the house of prayer; but you have made it a den of thieves' (St. Luke xix.).

It is possible to find people unhappy enough to go to church, not to adore their Lord, but to show themselves off, meet their acquaintance, or from some similar motives. And there are others who indulge wilful distraction, are irreverent in manner, stare about, try to distract others, and cherish sinful thoughts in their hearts. Are not all these making 'My house a den of thieves'? Are they not robbing God of His glory?

Let me take care never to be reckoned among such offenders; but ever with trembling, yet loving, awe, let me enter the 'house of sacrifice,' saying to myself. 'The place whereon thou standest is holy ground' (Exodus iii.).

Third Point.

'But Jesus said to them, Yea, have ye never read, Out of the mouths of babes and sucklings Thou hast perfected praise?' (St. Matt. xxi.)

This answer our Lord gave to the angry priests and scribes, who had asked Him, as the Hosanna of the clear childish voices rang through the Temple, 'Hearest Thou what these say?' What a joy for the young to think that children rendered our Blessed Lord meet homage!

The Church has treasured up the memory of their deed, and every Palm Sunday she sings,

'Glory and praise to Thee, Redeemer blest,
To whom their glad Hosannas children poured.'

Our Lord, then, will not despise our little offerings, little prayers, and little services. He doth not despise 'little days,' says the prophet. Let no one ever say, 'I am too young, or too stupid, or too obscure to do anything for God;' but rather let each say with holy David, 'I am little and despised, but I have not forgotten Thine ordinances' (Ps. cxviii.).

Colloquy.—Resolution.

February 25.

SATURDAY AFTER FIRST SUNDAY IN LENT— THE BARREN FIG-TREE.

First Prelude.—Imagine you see the fig-tree by which our Lord stood.

Second Prelude.—Grant, O Lord, that I may bring forth fruit unto life everlasting.

'And the next day, when they came from Bethania, He was hungry.'

When we read of our dear Lord suffering from hunger, do we not wish we could have been there, that we might have supplied His wants? Do we not feel that we could have borne hunger ourselves, or rather not have felt it, if He would have deigned to accept food from us? But He is hungry still; He says so with His own divine lips: 'I was hungry, and ye gave Me to eat;' for 'as long as you did it to one of these My least brethren, you did it to Me.' If, then, I help another, I am feeding Jesus Christ.

Second Point.

'And when He had seen afar off a fig-tree having leaves, He came, if perhaps He might find anything on it' (St. Mark xi.).

How easily were our Lord's wants satisfied! A few figs were all He would have taken to sustain Him for His long day's labour in the Temple.

And I find so many things necessary for my comfort; I am so ready to complain of privation.

Third Point.

'And when He was come to it, He found nothing but leaves' (St. Mark xi.).

How sad it seems to us that our Lord should have found nothing on the tree, when He was in need of food! But is not this fig-tree a picture of those who show their devotion in outward practices of piety, but who will not overcome themselves, and therefore bring not forth fruit? 'The fruit of the Spirit is charity, joy, peace, patience, mildness, modesty.'

Those who are pious outwardly, but who do not guard their tongues, their eyes, their tempers, and passions, are like trees with 'nothing but leaves;' and it will be with them as it was with the fig-tree, which presently 'withered away.'

Colloquy.—Resolution.

FEBRUARY 26.

SECOND SUNDAY IN LENT—THE PASCH.

First Prelude.—Imagine you see the upper

chamber where our Lord and His Apostles met.

Second Prelude.—Create in me a clean heart, O God.

First Point.

'And the day of unleavened bread came, on which it was necessary the Pasch should be killed' (St. Luke xxii.).

The Pasch, or eating of the Paschal lamb, was the greatest feast the Jews had, and it was the greatest type of the Messias, the true Lamb of God who was to come.

The last time for celebrating this feast had arrived; after this day the Pasch would be of no avail before God. Our Lord chose to fulfil the law to the last moment, and to assemble His community or family, His chosen twelve, to eat the Pasch together. That night so many centuries back the Lord had destroyed all the first-born of Egypt, because the Egyptians would not let His chosen people go; and now He was about to sacrifice

His own and only Son, that we might be 'delivered from the power of darkness.'

Second Point.

'The Master saith, Where is the refectory where I may eat the Pasch with My disciples? And he will show you a large dining-room furnished' (St. Mark xiv.).

Pilgrims to the Holy Land describe the cœnacle or supper-room as a large hall, with vaulted roof supported by two pillars, and here were the table that was about to be consecrated for evermore, and the couches for the guests. The place has been so often painted, it is easy to bring an idea of it before our minds, and, as we know, this upper chamber was about to be the scene of the 'Last Supper.'

Let us ask ourselves whether our hearts are fit dwelling-places for Him. For He was then about to bestow upon us a means by which we might 'dwell in Him and He in us.'

Third Point.

'Now there was leaning on Jesus' bosom one of the disciples whom Jesus loved.'

The mode of Eastern nations, even to the present day, at meals, is to recline on a sort of couch, which is placed by the side of the table. It was thus that St. John could lean on the bosom of the Lord. It seems to us a great privilege; but our Lord was about to give a far greater one to us.

St. John lay on His Sacred Heart; but that very Heart comes to lie on mine and to fill me with His love. I am no longer invited to the Paschal feast once in the year, but to feed continually on the 'Lamb without spot' offered up for me.

'What shall I render unto the Lord for all the things that He hath rendered unto me?' (Ps. cxv.)

Colloquy.—Resolution.

February 27.

Monday after Second Sunday in Lent—Our Lord washes His Disciples' Feet.

First Prelude.—Imagine you see the upper chamber.

Second Prelude.—Wash me, O Lord, in Thy Precious Blood.

First Point.

'He riseth from supper, layeth aside His garments, and having taken a towel, girded Himself. After that He putteth water in a basin, and began to wash the feet of the disciples, and to wipe them with the towel wherewith He was girded' (St. John xiii.).

Let us contemplate well this wonderful picture of humility: our Lord making Himself the servant of His Apostles, and performing one of the most lowly offices one human creature can render to another.

Can I ever say that anything I am asked to do is below me, when I think of my Lord and my God washing the feet of His Apostles, poor rough uneducated men?

Second Point.

'Peter saith to Him, Thou shalt never wash my feet. Jesus answered him, If I wash thee not, thou shalt have no part in Me' (St. John xiii.).

It was more than the impetuous Peter could bear. His thoughts were all of the glory and dignity of his Master. He had not learnt yet the lesson of His deep humility. He did not realise his own sinfulness, and that it was only because his Master 'emptied Himself, taking the form of a servant' (Phil. ii.), that he had any hope of eternal life.

When I am proud, shrinking from blame or reproof, let me remember that it is only because my sinless Lord 'humbled Himself' that the kingdom of heaven was opened to me, and that none can enter save those who follow His example.

Third Point.

'Simon Peter saith to Him, Lord, not only my feet, but also my hands and my head. Jesus saith to him, He that is washed needeth not but to wash his feet, but is clean wholly' (St. John xiii.).

These words show us that our Lord requires purity of soul before we approach Holy Communion. Our Lord added, 'Ye are clean, but not all,' meaning the unhappy Judas.

How careful we should, then, be to cleanse our souls frequently in the Sacrament of Penance, that we may be able to make worthy Communions! The special grace of frequent confession is purity of soul. Am I trying to become more and more pure in our Lord's eyes?

Colloquy.—Resolution.

February 28.

TUESDAY AFTER SECOND SUNDAY IN LENT— THE SAME (CONTINUED).

First Prelude.—Same as yesterday.

Second Prelude.—Jesus, meek and humble of Heart, make my heart like unto Thine.

First Point.

'Then after He had washed their feet and taken His garments they sat down again' (St. John xiii.).

He had then washed the feet not only of His faithful eleven, but of the traitor and the thief. Perhaps no two crimes excite so much scorn and contempt from men as those of which Judas was guilty—a mean pilfering from the bag which contained the alms given to the community, and the base betrayal of his Master while pretending to be still His disciple. Yet our dear Lord did not repulse him, but washed those guilty feet, yearning over him with unutterable love.

What a lesson of patience and forgiveness! How can I, a miserable sinful creature, ever dare to cherish a resentment or a grudge, ever dare to withhold a full and free forgiveness?

Second Point.

'If I, then, being your Lord and Master, have washed your feet, you ought also to wash one another's feet' (St. John xiii.).

The Church obeys these words of our Lord literally, and on Thursday in Holy Week every Bishop, beginning with the Pope himself, publicly washes the feet of twelve men chosen for the purpose; and even when this solemn act is performed by the prelate in rich vestments, surrounded by state and ceremony, the lowliness of the deed, and the vivid realisation it brings before the mind of the wondrous humility of our Incarnate God, fill the souls of those who witness it with love and gratitude.

But our Lord meant us to do more than literally obey His words. He meant us to be ready for humble lowly offices; and if, by position, we are set above others, to be ready when occasion permits to abase ourselves below all.

Third Point.

'For I have given you an example, that as I have done to you, so you do also' (St. John xiii.).

The Saints have pondered over these words, and then we see them washing lepers, waiting on the sick in hospitals, begging for alms whereby to relieve the poor, and bearing the scorn and ridicule of men with joy.

Am I glad to do anything that the world calls menial if I am able? Do I try, at least sometimes, to take the lowest place for love of Him who for love of me washed His disciples' feet?

Colloquy.—Resolution.

February 29.

**WEDNESDAY AFTER SECOND SUNDAY IN LENT—
JUDAS ISCARIOT.**

First Prelude.—Imagine you see the streets of Jerusalem.

Second Prelude.—Lead me not into temptation, but deliver me from evil.

First Point.

'Judas Iscariot who was the traitor' (St. Luke vi.).

Such is the terrible title by which one of the chosen twelve is known, and his history is to be to us an everlasting warning that there is no position so high, or so secure, but that he who holds it may fall. We learn by it to 'work out our salvation in fear and trembling' (Phil. ii.), never presuming on our graces and privileges; and we learn also never to be discouraged if those we have had reason to respect and to look up to should unhappily come to fall.

Our Lord has said, ' It must needs be that

scandals come ; but nevertheless, woe to that man by whom the scandal cometh' (St. Matt. xviii.).

Second Point.

'Why was not this ointment sold for three hundred pence, and given to the poor? Now he said this, not because he cared for the poor, but because he was a thief' (St. John xii.).

We see, then, that Judas Iscariot did not become bad all at once. Little by little his sin grew upon him : first he, the follower of Jesus, the great model of poverty, began to love money ; then he began to pilfer; to conceal his fault he lied, and became a hypocrite. He, the secret thief, sat in judgment and condemned the generous Magdalene. So he fell lower and lower, till at last we see him creeping along the streets of Jerusalem to the house of Caiphas, where the enemies of our Lord were gathered together ; and we hear him say, ' What will you give me, and I will deliver Him unto you ?' (St. Matt. xxvi.)

Have I any besetting sin? any fault that masters me—that it seems too hard to overcome? Even so let me never lose courage nor patience. If I do not despair I shall win.

Third Point.

'To take the place from which Judas hath by transgression fallen' (Acts i.). Fifty days after that terrible night on which Judas had betrayed his Lord, his place was filled up— 'another took his bishopric' (Ps. cviii.).

He had not succeeded in destroying the work of Jesus Christ, but only in destroying himself. We learn by this not to be dismayed or terrified when we hear of powerful enemies of the Church, or apostasies among those who were in her foremost ranks. They make a great noise for a while, and then they pass away, others take their places, others wear their crowns.

Am I careless about my graces? Do I make too sure of my eternal crown?

'He that thinketh he standeth, let him

take heed lest he fall' (1 Cor. x.). 'Merciful and gracious Lord, give to me, I beseech Thee, the most necessary of all things—true humility and perseverance in Thy service to the end of my life.'

Colloquy.—Resolution.

March 17.

FEAST OF ST. PATRICK, APOSTLE OF IRELAND.

First Prelude.—Imagine you see St. Patrick in glory.

Second Prelude.—Blessed Apostle, pray for me.

First Point.

' Ireland, which had up to that time been given over to the service of idols, was by the preaching of Patrick so wrought upon, that she soon brought forth the fruit which won her the name of the Island of Saints.'*

St. Patrick, therefore, had a special glory

* Roman Breviary.

given to few even of the Saints. He was an apostle, for he converted a whole nation to God.

How we, then, should rejoice in his great gifts and glory, and how earnestly we should seek his intercession!

Second Point.

'He was a great practiser of lowliness, and after the example of the Apostle, he always continued to work with his own hands.'*

Let me learn from this never to despise lowly laborious employments, because it is a great means to help us to attain humility, and let me be ever diligent at my appointed task.

Third Point.

'He bent his knees to God in worship three hundred times every day, and he made on himself the sign of the Cross a hundred times at each of the seven hours.'*

And thus he left confidence in prayer and

° Roman Breviary.

patience under the Cross as an undying heritage to the people whom he loved so much.

Am I cultivating these two great virtues? Colloquy.—Resolution.

March 19.

FEAST OF ST. JOSEPH, HUSBAND OF OUR LADY.

First Prelude.—Imagine you see St. Joseph in glory.

Second Prelude.—Help me, I beseech Thee, O Lord, for the sake of the husband of Thy Holy Mother.

First Point.

'Joseph, her husband, being a just man' (St. Matt. i.).

With what perfect self-abnegation and devotion did St. Joseph perform his office as the guardian of Mary! With what tender care he watched over her, laboured for her! He shared her joys and he suffered in her sorrows. He did not live to see the last four of her Dolours. The Saints have supposed that the agony of witnessing the Passion was spared to him, for his tender heart would have broken with grief.

When I want protection, when I am in trouble, let me go to St. Joseph.

> 'Thou wert a shadow thrown
> From the Father's summit lone,
> Over Mary's life to lie ;
> O, be thy shadow cast
> O'er our present and our past ;
> Dearest of Saints, be near us when we die.'[c]

Second Point.

'Thy father and I have sought Thee' (St. Luke ii.).

It was given to St. Joseph to be the foster-father of Jesus, to render Him all those services a father gives to a child. He carried Him in his arms, and the Sacred Heart beat close to the heart of Joseph. He laboured for Him in His childhood. He fed and sheltered his God, and watched over Him with

[c] Father Faber.

unceasing vigilance. What, then, shall be his reward from Him who says that if we give a cup of cold water in His Name we shall not lose our reward?

> 'Thou wert guardian of the Lord,
>   Foster-father of the Word,
> Who in thy arms did lie;
>   If we His brothers be,
>   We are foster-sons to thee;
> Dearest of Saints, be near us when we die.'

Third Point.

'A faithful man shall abound with blessings' (Prov. xxviii.).

One of the many blessings bestowed on St. Joseph was that he died in the arms of Jesus and Mary.

We long to have a priest by our deathbed. The great High-Priest stood by St. Joseph's dying couch. We ask our Lady to pray for us at the hour of our death, but St. Joseph's head was supported by her virginal hands. Happy Saint, what bliss was thine! Faithful unto death, he had gained a crown of of life (Apoc. ii.).

> ' When thy gentle years were run
> On the bosom of thy Son
> Like an infant didst thou lie ;
> O, by thy happy death
> In that tranquil Nazareth,
> Dearest of Saints, be near us when we die.'

Colloquy.—Resolution.

www.ingramcontent.com/pod-product-compliance
Lightning Source LLC
Chambersburg PA
CBHW032148160426
43197CB00008B/823